The History
of Pascualete

The Countess of Romanones

THE HISTORY
OF PASCUALETE

The Countess of Romanones

KEEDICK PRESS • NEW YORK

To My Mother

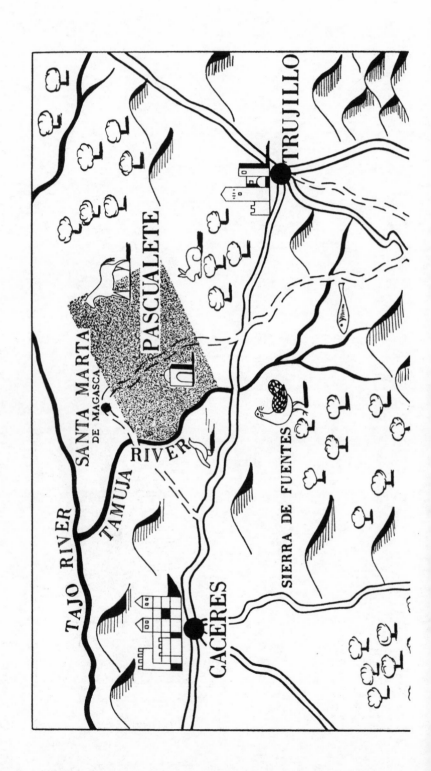

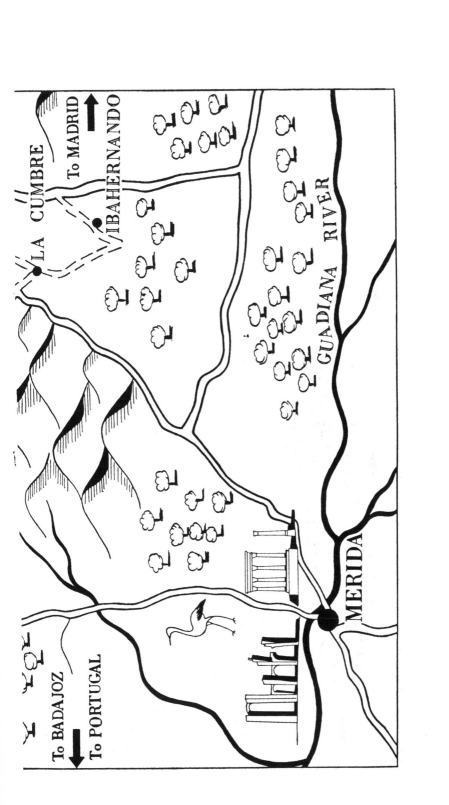

Contents

vii

Contents

PART ONE

THE DISCOVERY OF PASCUALETE

I

From America to Spain

I T W A S L O V E at first sight and I will never know why. There below me lay the grey barren fields of the plateau region just outside Madrid, not a ray of sunlight brightened the menacing snow-covered peaks of the Guadarramas. Although the world outside was at war on that bleak day of February 1944, a feeling of peace and aloofness reigned down there below where I was about to begin my job as a member of the American OSS. I clutched at my bag to reassure myself that I had my passport and papers, and once again I was filled with apprehension that despite all my training and instruction, I would not be worthy of the mission which had been entrusted to me. One of the two other passengers in the great empty airplane touched me on the arm to warn me to tighten my seat belt and we landed amidst a storm of dust and wind. I stepped out into the chilly, inhospitable air—out into a completely unknown world. I knew not a soul in that formidable country and I was barely twenty-two years old, but I was to spend the rest of my life there. I was to marry a Spaniard, and become so attached to this land that eventually I would live in an ancient house haunted by seven centuries of ancestors in a remote province of Spain. I would know that particular world in a manner more intimate than most Spaniards have ever done. That is the story I want to tell.

*   *   *

I was born in Pearl River, New York, the eldest of six children. My father and mother had been born there, too, and that is as far back as our town goes. Pearl River began when my mother's father, Grandfather Dexter, decided to build his new factory there, some time at the end of the last century. It was a quiet little village where everyone knew and worried about everyone else. There were no Grand Unions or supermarkets then. Just Rowan's butcher's shop, Schumacher's grocery store, the National Bank, Sandford's drugstore and the school—Main Street and Central Avenue. That was my world for seventeen years.

We lived on top of one of the two hills that formed the town, and grandfather's factory and the railroad track were down in the valley. From my bedroom window I could look down the hill to the train as it whistled by twice in the morning and twice at night on its way to and from New York. There was nowhere else for it to go.

In Pearl River even most of the houses were alike, built of shingles and stucco, with a porch tacked on one side or another, each house separated from the other by a lawn. In the winter there was plenty of snow and two big hills to sleigh down and in the spring the woods were thick with dragon flowers, violets and Jack-in-the-pulpit.

Nothing ever changed. Some of my schoolteachers had taught my mother years before. Nobody ever did anything very bad either. I suppose the few who did left town when they were ready to give vent to their inhibitions so that we missed all the fun.

When I was twelve years old a spinster schoolteacher of my mother's, who now lived on a farm near Albany (the capital of New York State), invited me to visit her. I had grown tall and skinny with bony knees and there seemed little hope for my looks. My grandmother was especially distressed when she looked at my olive skin and dark brown hair and eyes, she would sigh deeply and shake her head, saying:

'What a pity for a girl to be as dark as a gipsy!'

After a lot of discussion as to whether or not I should be allowed to go—Miss Donellan might not recognize me as she had not seen me since I was four—I was eventually put on the bus for Albany.

I remember the trip as one of the most fascinating experiences I had ever known. I tried to sit quietly in my seat as I had been told, but I soon forgot all my promises and found myself talking a mile a minute to the very nice lady next to me. When my questions seemed to have tired my neighbour, I tried them on other members of the bus and by the time we reached Albany I knew everyone who had made the trip with me intimately. The feeling of being alone in a world of so many nice people was thoroughly exhilarating. I decided then that when I was grown up somehow I would travel far, far away.

When it came time to go to college, I would have preferred a co-educational school with football games and dances, but my parents chose Mount St. Vincent's-on-the-Hudson, a Catholic girls' school with lights out at ten o'clock. But at least it was different from Pearl River and there were girls from as far away as Canada.

On December 7, 1941, I was spending the week-end at home from college. We had a maid then who insisted on keeping her hat on when she served at table.

'You must call her by her full last name—Mrs. Duffy,' my mother warned. 'And be careful to keep her happy because it is terribly difficult these days to get any help at all.'

Mrs. Duffy completely tyrannized the household and obliged us to have lunch and dinner at hours convenient to her.

That Sunday, as we were seated at table, the noise of Mrs. Duffy's radio going full blast in the kitchen seemed louder than usual. I could see that mother was just about to complain when Mrs. Duffy burst into the room with her hat completely askew and her hands gripping her head in despair. And that is how we learned that Japanese planes had just bombed Pearl Harbor.

My father looked at my mother, who remained speechless and nobody stirred for a few moments. We were thinking of Dexter and Tommy who were both away at college and who we knew would enlist as soon as they heard the news. And I was thinking of my date at Annapolis, my cadet at West Point and all the other boys who had made up my life and who tomorrow would be on their way to war. We knew that from then on our lives would be

5

changed, but I never thought that my own personal life would be so drastically affected.

A year later, after graduating from college, I tried every possible means to get overseas with the war effort, but no one would offer posts abroad to girls under twenty-five.

One night, at a dinner party in New York, I met a man who had just returned from Europe and who seemed very interested when we girls began complaining that all our brothers were overseas and we had to stay behind in America. We wanted to make some contribution comparable to theirs.

After dinner, the visitor took me aside. 'If you really are serious about working abroad,' he said, 'I think I can help you. I warn you, everyone thinks it would be interesting and even glamorous to be near the skirmish, but it's a far cry from what you might imagine. No matter where you go, you will find tragedy and misery and it isn't so easy for a young girl, accustomed to gaiety and comfort, to face the bitter realities of wartime.'

Somehow I convinced him that I meant it, and before parting he took my name and address and warned me not to tell anyone about our conversation.

Two months later, back in Pearl River, my father mentioned that he had heard from various friends in town that the FBI (Federal Bureau of Investigation) had been making inquiries about the family. My parents naturally assumed that it was because my brothers had been assigned to some secret mission. But I suspected that my friend was indeed keeping his promise.

Not long afterwards I received a letter from the War Department stating that I would be contacted by their representative. At the hour mentioned in the letter a man telephoned me with instructions to appear at an address in New York where I would receive further information. There they told me I had been accepted for a training course to prepare me for some special work.

My orders were to be in Washington, D.C., the following Monday. I was to travel under a false name and with a suitcase of simple country clothes from which all labels had been cut off. Any initials or paper with my name and address should be carefully removed from my person before making the trip. I was given an address and telephone number in Washington where my parents could contact me if necessary and I was to tell them that I had accepted a position with the War Department, but no more.

My mother was against it, of course. Anything that took me more than an hour away from Pearl River was sheer wickedness in her mind. But I got there, thanks to my father, who could usually be wheedled over to my side.

I waited patiently in the busy hallway in Washington until a young woman came and directed me to an office at the end of the corridor. I had no idea whom I was going to see, but as I walked in I recognized behind the desk the man I had met at the dinner party in New York. His warm handshake reassured me and he asked me to sit down.

'There is nothing I can tell you today about your work. The most I can do is to warn you to be very careful never to say anything about yourself. You are going to be tested in many ways to see how you adapt to new situations. From now on no one can know anything about you, whether you are American or European, whether you have lived in one country or another. Your success depends entirely on yourself and your ability to learn and to preserve secrecy.'

He picked up a long, narrow slip of yellow paper which he handed to me.

'Here are your instructions. You are not to arrive at your destination by taxi. Remember—you may be followed every moment from now on.'

As I walked out of the building I tried to memorize the words on the paper. 'Proceed to the Hotel Adams and wait until a black Chevrolet with licence number TX 24168 appears, at which time you will say to the driver, "Is this Mr. Tom's car?"'

My adventures had begun!

That evening I found myself in an old building somewhere in the country outside Washington, with a group of people looking just as bewildered as I. A man was apparently about to brief us.

7

The Discovery of Pascualete

'Well,' he said. 'You're probably wondering where you are and what you are here for, and I'm here this evening to tell you just that.'

He paused and looked us all over. He seemed to enjoy the state of suspense he was creating. He slowly got up and walked round his desk so as to be nearer to us and then, nonchalantly placing his hands behind him on the table top, he leaned back. His glance took us all in as he began to speak again.

'You are in the first school of espionage in the United States of America and you are here to be made into spies.'

A shiver ran up my spine, and Pearl River was far, far behind.

One night many months later I was looking down from the pilot's cabin of a Pan American Clipper where below hundreds and thousands of little sparkling lights formed myriad designs. That was Lisbon and my first view of Europe.

From then on, as a member of the OSS., the Office of Strategic Services, my name for all espionage purposes was 'Butch' or number 527. That very night I found myself in a cellar where I was introduced to several agents and briefed on the activities between Madrid and Lisbon organizations. I sat quietly in the corner of a smoky room listening to these men. Every now and then I would hear something like:

'What a pity poor old Joe got bumped off last week on the frontier. Those damn Nazis never do anything in a nice way. He was found with his throat slit.'

'Poor old Joe, indeed,' I thought. Where was I going to fit into this incredible world of cloak and dagger?

I did not know a word of Spanish, but I had majored in French in college. The OSS. had warned me I had only six months to master the language. If I failed, they would transfer me to another post.

From the first moment I decided not to waste five minutes with my fellow Americans. Most of my friends in the beginning

8

were very poor since my work brought me into contact with our agents who crossed the frontier or trailed German suspects inside the country. The food I first sampled was often difficult to swallow because it smelled strongly of fried, unrefined, green olive oil and the homes I first knew were unheated and reached by climbing a rickety flight of old steps or by a wobbly ancient elevator. But the people were gay and warm and through their enthusiasm I got to like everything Spanish, even the olive oil, and best of all none of them spoke English and my Spanish improved by leaps and bounds.

After a month, I took my first class in Spanish. I thought my professor would be impressed with the enormous progress I had already made. When I explained to him that I had been there only a month, instead of congratulating me for having learned so much so rapidly, he tapped his head and in an anguished voice said:

'Señorita, in all my life I have never heard my language so thoroughly abused.' After overcoming his original shock, he said sternly, 'Now, you must listen and repeat after me the following, "*Yo pido vino fino*".'

That was my only lesson in Spanish. But since I wanted desperately to stay in Spain, I went ahead making Spanish friends and in three months I managed to speak it almost as well as I do today.

The next year and a half was packed with excitement—planning drops of agents behind enemy lines and sitting up at night waiting for their radio contacts (if they came through); trailing suspects and making friends for the purpose of recruiting valuable foreign agents; hiding the brave French and Spanish women who sneaked across the Pyrenees to bring us vital battle order movements.

Whenever I got into trouble, the Spaniard's extraordinary courtesy and gallantry came to my rescue. Only a month after arriving I found myself in jail in Málaga, but I was soon released by a kind old police chief who at my departure presented me with a large bouquet of red carnations and his apologies for having kept an American señorita in an ugly cell for two nights.

The Discovery of Pascualete

I did not have much time for boy friends during the war but shortly after it was over I met an attractive young Spaniard called Luis. He had a lot of other names, too, but I never could remember them. He was blond and green-eyed and spoke English beautifully. We discovered that we both loved bullfights and he used to invite me on Sundays to watch the incomparable Manolete in the Madrid bullring. For two months I broke my dinner engagements on Sunday evenings, thinking that certainly this time Luis would ask me to have dinner with him after the fight, but each time he simply dropped me at my door and made an appointment for the following *corrida*.

Eventually he telephoned me during the week and asked me to dinner. But when he called for me he was accompanied by his two sisters with their husbands and thus our friendship continued chaperoned by the family all the time and only bullfights alone.

One day we were invited to a friend's ranch near Madrid where there was a small bullring and *aficionados* were allowed to try their skill with young bulls. I heard someone mention that a young German countess whom I knew to be a member of the SS during the war had fought at this same ranch several times very courageously. For some reason I wanted to show that an American girl could do as well.

After passing the small bull twice, I became very cocky about my prowess and dared to kneel down in imitation of the *pases de rodilla* that I had seen in the big rings. The first time the bull was kind and passed me by as he should. I looked up to see if Luis was fully appreciating my bravery and skill and for one brief moment forgot that the animal could turn quickly. I was trampled under his feet as he came back.

As I was dragged out of the ring, I heard Luis say, 'I think you had better marry me and stop doing such silly things.' I agreed, and my life as an American woman came to an abrupt end.

*   *   *

From America to Spain

During the first months of our marriage we travelled extensively and when we finally returned to Madrid to set up our house, it was something of a shock to notice that my husband did not rush to an office every morning.

In fact, for a long time, I rather suspected no office existed since our time seemed quite taken up with shooting parties, golf games and trips to the different country estates of his unlimited relatives.

Imagine my surprise and relief when one day Luis announced that the following morning he had to spend a few hours in his office. But these visits turned out to be few and far between and my American business sense made me wonder just how long our comfortable and leisurely life could continue.

One day, when I could stand it no longer, I said, 'Luis, do tell me something about your business interests.'

He looked as shocked as if I had accused him of robbing a bank.

'My dear,' he eyed me severely for the first time in our married life, 'Spanish wives do not mix in their husbands' business activities.'

But with a bit of prodding, Luis finally informed me that his income was derived principally from several large estates in southern and south-western Spain. This was all news to me and seemed infinitely more fascinating than a business in an office.

'But, Luis, how are you able to make any money from properties you never visit?'

He then patiently explained that in Spain large farms or ranches, usually referred to as *fincas*, are often worked by tenant farmers who once yearly, loaded with money bags and their accounts, make the trip to wherever the owner lives to pay their annual rent.

'But if we ran these *fincas* ourselves, wouldn't they bring in a larger income?' I ventured.

He quickly demolished that idea. 'Why should we work ourselves to death living in isolated country areas to make money which we would then not have time to spend? I do not like farming anyway and we Spaniards try to enjoy life. Even our poorest country workmen, once they have made enough money to pay for their simple needs, are not willing to work an extra hour. Do you really think it makes such a difference if we have three cars or one—as long as we are happy?'

The sheer logic of this thoroughly Latin philosophy completely stumped me.

Two more years went by. I was busy having babies and so absorbed in learning about Spain and its fascinating inhabitants that my initial curiosity about our properties was left unsatisfied, but not forgotten.

The final impetus came one day at a luncheon, when a friend of Luis' family said to me, 'Aline, you are so lucky. I've just come back from a trip to Estremadura. It is the most wonderful part of Spain—so wild, so romantic, so old-fashioned. The last vestige of what Spain was like hundreds of years ago! And it seems to me the olives are bigger, the sheep are fatter, the sky is bluer and the shooting is better than in any part of Spain. Yes, you really are fortunate.'

'Fortunate?' I asked. 'Me? But why do you say that?'

'Because Luis has some of the best *fincas* in that part of Spain. How I envy you having those marvellous properties.'

That did it. Now I was determined to visit those properties and see at least one tree that was responsible for our comfortable existence.

When I told Luis about this conversation, he scoffed, 'Why, that man is insane. What does he mean? Estremadura is the poorest, the most backward, the most uncivilized part of Spain. And what is more, the *fincas* are located in isolated areas with no roads leading to them. You would probably have to travel part of the way by donkey.'

He also added that neither his mother nor his grandmother had ever visited them and he saw no reason for me to begin. I pointed out that perhaps in the past fifty years new roads might have been built, but he assured me it was unlikely in those particular parts of Spain. Finally, his patience hanging by a shred, he said, 'Very well, if you insist on this mad idea of yours, then go and talk with my business administrator, José Silva. It will give him quite a shock, as he has been working for our family for forty-five years and has never had to deal with a woman yet. But he is kind and patient and I suppose he will give you whatever information you want.'

So I appeared the next morning in Luis' offices where a fat, short, owl-eyed little man was awaiting me. Don José immediately fell into the stilted, old-fashioned third person always used by subordinates in Spain.

'What an honour to have the Señora Condesa gracing our office this morning! What can I do for the Señora Condesa? I am at her service.' He beamed and smiled as he directed me to a chair.

'I have come this morning, Don José, to learn something of my husband's business affairs and to make plans to visit certain of his *fincas*.'

Don José's face changed dramatically. He leaned forward and asked agitatedly, 'But is something wrong? Does the Señora Condesa not have confidence in my management?'

'Oh, heavens no, Don José,' I said quickly, aware that I probably had offended his Spanish pride. 'Don't misunderstand. It's just that sometimes we American women do take an interest in our husband's business affairs, even if it is only to give an occasional opinion.'

He shook his head from side to side mumbling to himself, 'This is certainly very strange, very strange.'

Then he got up and went to a filing cupboard and returned with a stack of papers.

'The Señor Conde,' he began, 'has several very nice *fincas* in Estremadura, the cattle and sheep raising district of Spain.'

'Where exactly is Estremadura?' I asked.

'It is in south-west Spain. To go there one takes the main road to Portugal.'

'Tell me, which of these properties could I visit?'

'Let me see. Well, the *fincas* in the province of Badajoz have no town near enough which provides comfortable accommodation, and they are too far away. Undoubtedly, the *finca* near Trujillo

The Discovery of Pascualete

called Pascualete would be the most convenient to visit. It is about one hundred and fifty miles from here. This *finca* your husband inherited in 1936 from his maternal grandfather, the Conde de Torre Arias, Marqués de Santa Marta, who owned some of the best properties in Estremadura.'

At the risk of seeming disloyal to my husband, I muttered something about not understanding why Luis had not taken more interest in these properties.

At that Don José's expression changed again, to a look of infinite sadness and gentleness.

'After all, the Señora Condesa must realize that the Señor Conde was only eight years old when his mother died, and although he then inherited his title of Quintanilla along with some properties, he obviously was not of an age when he could interest himself in them. And these properties actually were not finally settled until two years ago—so they have not been his for very long.

'Also, when he inherited *fincas* from his grandfather, Torre Arias, who was shot down by the Reds in the streets of Madrid during those first dreadful days of our Civil War, the Señor Conde was a mere child of sixteen.

'That was the last time I saw the Señor Conde until after the war. He escaped from Madrid to the northern part of Spain where he joined the Nationalist troops. Being under age, he enlisted using an assumed name and he lay many months, horribly wounded, in an improvised hospital near the front line trenches of Bilbao, without his family being aware of it. He had enlisted as a private and by the age of seventeen he was a first lieutenant.

'Do not think that our Spanish boys are lazy and uninterested in their country's welfare. Remember that as children they were exposed to the atrocities of a bitter Civil War. They were not even able to finish their education, nor did they have time to consider their own interests,' he concluded sadly.

However, I had to get back to the subject at hand. I informed Don José that I had already decided that I would visit the ranch he suggested—Pascualete.

From America to Spain

'Of course,' he replied. 'As the Señora Condesa wishes, but I feel it is my duty to warn the Señora Condesa that this is the most backward section of Spain. There are no comfortable places for you to stay overnight and the inns in these country towns provide miserable food—everything is cooked with rancid olive oil. It is not a place for a lady such as the Señora Condesa to travel in.'

I had heard all this before from Luis, who had gone further, saying there were no bathrooms, and my bed was likely to be filled with rats, bedbugs and cockroaches. Don José's warning did not impress me at all.

'Don't worry, Don José, I'll manage somehow.'

'Then I will advise someone from Pascualete to come to Trujillo to meet you. However, it will take at least four or five days for my letter to arrive and another week to receive an answer.'

'But I don't want to wait that long. Why not send a telegram?'

'Señora Condesa, a telegram and a letter are one and the same thing in that part of Spain. Either one would have to be delivered by donkey.'

The only way to present my proposed trip to the *finca* to Luis seemed to be to invite a few friends to go with us, talking it up as a mysterious and exciting trek in medieval Spain.

My great ally was the beautiful film star, Annabella, who, on various visits to Madrid had been urging me to make the trip with her, even if Luis did not go. Also corralled into the adventure were a couple from the Brazilian Embassy and one lone brave Spaniard.

Luis, who is basically easy-going and good humoured, finally decided to make the best of it and go along, muttering that he could not allow his wife to face the hazards of such a reckless journey alone.

'I suppose I should have realized that when I married an American my life would be turned upside down,' he added.

I had already learned that being an American is a tremendous advantage in tradition-bound Spain. Any unorthodox notion was immediately attributed to this unfortunate accident of birth.

2

Journey into the Unknown

THE DAY for our excursion arrived. By this time I felt we were about to discover the North Pole, and it hardly seemed possible our route was only a three-and-a-half-hour motor trip on the main highway to Portugal.

But as we left Madrid with its bustling, thriving modern life, we gradually put the twentieth century behind us. We passed vast treeless fields; there was little traffic on the roads, only a rare petrol station and infrequent small villages.

Often, a flock of sheep casually crossing our path would slow us down and the women on their knees doing the family wash on the banks of some little stream would lift their heads as we passed and wave gaily to us. Each little village, with its white-washed houses squeezed side by side, had a picturesque water fountain in the town square. There the village women gathered, their graceful clay water jugs balanced precariously on their heads. The octagonal church, dominating each village and with the ever-present stork in its belfry, had not changed since the Middle Ages.

As our road twisted down a hill around the yellowed stone walls of the castle of Maqueda, we were already back in the era of knights in armour, when noblemen built austere fortresses to protect their families from the marauding Moors. Along our route thirteenth-century castles and watchtowers appeared frequently, perched high on the mountain peaks.

Two hours out of Madrid, we were already in Estremadura. All nature seemed brighter in colour and more savage in contour. Forests of cork trees and evergreen oaks were interspersed with wide fields of crimson poppies spread out like immense oriental carpets before our eyes. And framing this dramatic picture were the towering purple peaks of the Gredos Mountains outlined against the incredibly blue sky.

With a captive audience, Luis suddenly became expansive, and gave us a running commentary sprinkled with historical anecdotes. And he began to chide me.

'How is it that an intelligent American girl, with a college education, knows nothing about the province of Estremadura—the most important province in Spain, historically speaking, for the Americans?'

I looked bewildered, for I really had never heard of it until I came to Spain.

'Don't you know that this province produced most of the famous conquistadores? Francisco Pizarro, who discovered Peru, was born in Trujillo and from a near-by village came Hernan Cortes, who helped make the early history of Mexico and Santo Domingo. And you must have read in your history books about Balboa, who crossed the Isthmus of Panama and discovered the Pacific Ocean! He came from here too. There were hundreds of these tough, hardy men, bred in this dry, harsh climate with its unyielding soil—these men could survive all difficulties—and that is why they managed so well in the New World. Of course, they sent or brought their wealth back to Trujillo and built palaces and founded noble houses. So you see, this town we are approaching was a prosperous, bustling metropolis of the sixteenth century.'

The sun had just begun to set as we looked up and saw a fortified medieval city perched high on a peak of slate rock. It looked like a jagged granite island rising out of a sea of black, barren plains. Silhouetted against the pink and blue sunset were the intriguing shapes of Arab towers, an enormous castle and massive crenellated stone walls.

'There it is,' said Luis. 'That's Trujillo.' And I even detected a note of excitement in his voice.

Our car could barely manoeuvre the twisting narrow cobble-stoned streets which took us up a steep hill towards the main

17

The Discovery of Pascualete

plaza of Trujillo. Although I had visited a number of old cities in Spain—Toledo, Salamanca, Granada—I had never seen one like Trujillo, so isolated and now, as the sun was setting, so eerie with its strange shadows. Every now and then a figure shrouded in black stepped back from the path of our car and pressed against a wall to let us by. Lining the street, on either side, stood immense granite palaces, jutting up into the sky and blotting out the last rays of the sun.

We burst from the steep alley on to a broad spacious plaza, surrounded by ancient arcades and noble stone buildings. Above the plaza we could see clusters of towers, old chimneys and weathered tile roofs, huddled one above the other on the hillside.

In the centre of the plaza brown-faced urchins were tossing pebbles into a fountain and dominating the entire picture was an enormous bronze statue of a man on horseback with a fancy plumed helmet, its shadow making weird patterns on the earth.

'That is Pizarro,' said Luis, pointing to the statue. 'It was done by Mrs. Huntington, the famous American sculptress, and donated by her to the city of Trujillo.'

Before we could pursue the subject further, we found ourselves surrounded by an army of jabbering happy-faced children dressed in brightly coloured rags. And inquisitive adults put their heads out of the tiny shops under the plaza's arcade.

As usual in Spain, we had arrived late. At the door of the little inn stood two men. One, obviously the innkeeper, was small and thin with sparse wisps of hair and a toothless grin. He wore a freshly starched white waiter's jacket which did not hide the grimy, collarless shirt underneath. His dark brown corduroy trousers, baggy and worn, were threadbare at the knees. As we approached, he bowed awkwardly and deeply from the waist, letting his arms hang limply at his sides. He seemed to know immediately who we were, for he addressed Luis.

'Señor Conde,' he repeated several times as he continued to bow.

The other figure intrigued me as he stood stiffly at attention. He looked about fifty years old and was wearing the typical

18

Primitivo

View of the
Plaza in Trujillo
with the statue
of Francisco
Pizarro

costume of Spanish country people—a coarse, dark blue cotton smock, with full gathered sleeves and a straight-brimmed hat. Grasped in both hands was a thick, home-made walking stick. An extraordinary expression of tranquillity and goodness shone from his dark-lashed, clear brown eyes lighting up his weather-beaten face.

This was Juan, who Luis explained was the *arrendatario* or the farmer who, with his three brothers, rented and worked all the land of the *finca*. Juan was the one who made the yearly trek to Madrid to pay the rent, so of course he knew Luis. Today he had come to Trujillo to direct us to the *finca*.

He took off his hat and bowed deeply and Luis shook hands with him and exchanged a few pleasantries. Annabella and I were giggling like schoolgirls and I said to her, eyeing the pathetic little inn, 'Remember, no matter what happens, we can't complain.'

We followed Juan and Luis into a hall. There, behind a small reception desk, stood a smiling, bespectacled man, trying hard to give the impression that customers for the Hotel Cubano appeared every moment. But the utter silence and dimness of the place made it apparent that for the time being we were the only visitors.

I heard Luis say to Juan, 'Just a minute. I will take care of the rooms and order dinner and then I will be right with you and introduce you to the rest of the party.'

A look of deep concern came over Juan's face and he asked, 'But Señor Conde, what is this about rooms in this miserable little inn when the *palacio* of the Senores Condes is awaiting them?'

Luis turned to Juan in amazement, as if he had not heard clearly.

'What are you talking about, Juan? What *palacio*?' And Juan, in truly dramatic Spanish style, replied with a flourish, 'What *palacio* other than Pascualete, the *palacio* of the ancestors of the Señores Condes, the oldest country *palacio* in this part of Spain.'

Annabella, who had some understanding of Spanish, said, 'What on earth is he saying, Aline? What's all this about a palace?'

Luis turned to her and said in English, 'Don't pay any attention

The Discovery of Pascualete

to that. You know how these country people will call anything a palace.'

But Juan continued, 'And Señor Conde, the people of Pascualete have been preparing for days for your arrival. Our women have been cooking all day.'

This was all Annabella and I needed.

'You can do as you like, Luis,' I said, 'but Annabella and I are going to the palace of your ancestors!'

And so we started on the road to Pascualete leaving behind us the desolate face of the innkeeper.

After thirteen kilometres on the main highway out of Trujillo, Juan told us to turn on a dirt cowpath to the right. By now it was a pitch black night, but Juan, with the penetrating eyes of country people, directed us round stones and trees we could not even see. Every so often we had to get out of the car and search for a way round some big rock, and all the while Luis was saying:

'Can't you see? This is absolute madness. No one in his right mind would start off on such a trip in the middle of the night. The cars are going to be ruined and actually it is my fault for permitting such an absurd trip. We could just as well have waited until morning.'

Hoping to get Luis' mind off his worries, I tried changing the subject. I had been observing Juan as he directed us, and I was distressed to see what seemed to me obvious evidence of poverty —his humble clothes, for example.

Speaking in English, I said to Luis, 'Look at this poor man. Really we must try to help him out a bit Luis—perhaps you could give him some of your clothes after we know him a bit better.'

Luis laughed so loudly that I was embarrassed and also I was shocked. How could he be so unfeeling?

'My dear, before you begin to play Lady Bountiful, I think I should tell you that 'this poor man', as you call him, probably has more money in the bank than I do. Do you know that the last time he came to Madrid to pay the rent he told me he had three million pesetas in the bank and wanted to invest it in something.'

Journey into the Unknown

This really staggered me, for as I quickly calculated it came to about $75,000.

'But Luis, he doesn't even wear a tie!'

'He does not think it necessary—and furthermore, the way to acquire money is not to waste it on foolishness—and he would regard a necktie as the worst sort of foolishness.'

It seemed hours before we finally were told to stop. (Actually, it was only eight kilometres on the cowpath.) The headlights of the car revealed a massive stone arch and underneath a crowd of men, women and children. Juan, who by this time had us completely in his power, escorted me out of the car and walked along beside me.

'Juan, what are all these people doing out here in the middle of the night?' I asked.

'The Señora Condesa does not realize that this is a very great day for us, for it must be way over a hundred years since anyone of the family of the Señor Conde has ever visited this *finca*. These people have been here all day waiting to meet, for the first time in their lives, the owners of Pascualete, where they and their ancestors have lived and worked for many generations.'

He added that many had never been further away than Trujillo and that neither in their lives nor in the time of their grandfathers had anyone laid eyes on the owners.

'There is one amongst us whose great-grandfather remembered, when he was only a small child, having spoken to the Marqués de Santa Marta one day when he was riding through Pascualete.'

Several oil lanterns lit up the crowd under the stone arch and as we approached a ray of light fell on a tall, lean man with a lined, dark, handsome face and a mop of unruly black hair. The bone structure clearly marked under the dark leathery skin and the piercing black eyes brought to mind the faces in El Greco's paintings. A crumpled hat was grasped in his hand and as we approached and were introduced, I was particularly impressed by his quiet air and dignity.

'This is Primitivo,' Juan explained, 'the guard of the Señores Condes. He was born here at Pascualete, as were his father and

The Discovery of Pascualete

his grandfather, all of whom have been the head guard of this ranch for many, many years.'

I was fascinated by his incredible name. Primitivo presented his wife, Maria, whose appearance, alas, was as plain as her husband's was dramatic. At first glance she seemed a colourless, nondescript woman with mouse-brown hair drawn severely back into a sparse bun. Neither fat nor thin, tall nor short, Maria wore a black baggy dress gathered at the waist by a large black apron.

All the group now came to be presented.

'Many of these people are shepherds, as this *finca* produces mostly sheep,' Juan explained to me. 'They live far away from the main house in straw huts, which we call *choʒos*, at the outposts of the *finca*. But they have been waiting many hours to see the Señores Condes.'

As one after the other passed in front of me, sweeping into deep low bows as they were presented, I began to feel like Catherine the Great. Juan explained about each person as he made the introduction:

'This is old Tia Isidora,' he would say. 'She lives right here on the patio and is very famous because she sews better than anyone else on the *finca*.'

Tia Isidora looked at me beaming and patting my hand and calling me the Señora Condesita (the little countess), a name which stuck with me for a long time.

'But we had no idea our Señora Condesita was going to be so young and pretty,' another said, which naturally won me over completely. As I made my way through the group, I overheard several remarks about my clothing. I was wearing a turtle-neck sweater and one old woman ventured that I must have something the matter with my throat.

'She looks a little thin,' I heard another say. 'I do not know how long she would last in our climate.'

Not one person moved from his place until I had finished, and then we passed through the arch and found ourselves in a spacious patio. From there we were shown up a twisting staircase into an enormous bare stone room with whitewashed walls, a vaulted ceiling and the biggest fireplace I had ever seen in my life.

A great stone canopy overhung the fireplace which stretched almost the entire width of the room. Underneath, on the walls, hung many skillets and copper pots, while two stone benches flanked either side of the hearth. Two women were kneeling in front of the open fire preparing our dinner. One was turning a heavy iron spit which held two sizzling sucking pigs whose drippings she poured every now and then into a pot of beans slowly simmering in one corner of the fire. As we walked across the floor of tiny coloured cobble-stones, they jumped up and then sank into dips or *reverencias* as these bows are called in Spanish.

They motioned us to the only pieces of furniture in the room— a large table covered with a heavy cloth which fell to the ground and several rustic chairs. We sat down and as I put my legs under the tablecloth I felt the most delicious, warm sensation and discovered that under the table were hot coals in a brazier—a marvellous substitute for central heat. This sort of table, Luis explained, is known as a *mesa camilla*.

As we began dinner, it was all we could do not to laugh, since each dish was presented to us with a deep bow and each guest addressed with a flowery title. Annabella was called the Señora Duquesa, our diplomatic friends became the Excellent Ambassadors (and ever since all our foreign friends have been so addressed) and our Spanish guest was assumed to be no less than a Principe. We teased Luis mercilessly.

'The nerve of you,' Annabella said, 'never telling Aline that you owned a palace—complete with loyal retainers!'

'Well,' he answered sceptically, 'I am still not convinced that there is much of a palace here. After all, we have only seen this room.'

That was all the cue we needed. Immediately, big lanterns were brought and, guided by Juan, we went back down the same stairs we had just climbed and out to the patio again. This time we turned and entered the first floor through large Spanish doors shaped like an arch. As if by a miracle, helping hands appeared out of the

The Discovery of Pascualete

night, doors were opened and shut for us and shadowy creatures flitted about to help.

We found ourselves in a large room with vaulted ceilings and many beautiful carved wooden doors fitted into massive stone arches.

'This is the entrance hall of the *palacio*,' Juan indicated, with a grand sweep of his hand.

The proportions were beautiful. There was no furniture and in the dim corners were big sacks and boxes, which Juan explained contained the wool, olive oil and other produce of the *finca*. As we walked along, my heels caught in the tiny cobblestones in the floor, and looking down, I noticed a strange pattern in the little stones.

'Juan, come closer with the lantern,' I said, pointing to the floor. 'What is this strange design?'

'Ah, Señora Condesa, that is the *escudo* of the *finca*. There are many, many copies of that *escudo* in Pascualete. That is the most important *escudo* in this part of the country!' he said proudly.

An *escudo* is a coat of arms, and looking closely I could distinguish clearly five black roses, four in a square and one below on a greyish background. In that dark room, with its strange smells and shadows, the *escudo* seemed like an authentic voice out of the past. Who was this nobleman who had placed his stamp even in the very floor of his palace?

Everyone came running to look at this discovery.

'Luis, do you recognize this *escudo*?' I asked.

He looked carefully. 'I have never seen it before. I do not think it can be from my family. Do you know anything about it, Juan?'

'All I know, Señor Conde, is that it has been here as long as this house has been here and who knows how long that may be. I am not a learned man, but even I can tell that many people's grandfathers have lived and died here and this house has been here before all of them.'

Having delivered himself of this weighty speech, Juan picked up the lantern and led us ahead into a series of similar rooms. There were no halls, but as we walked from one room to another, I

24

noticed the interior walls were at least five feet thick and solid stone. And it seemed to me the house was all on different levels. We went up a few steps to one room, then down again, then up again.

In one room, I stopped to inspect the windows. Instead of being square, like most windows, they were all arched, with carved wooden shutters. As I tried to open the shutters I was overwhelmed to see the depth of the window sill. It was really like a window seat, deeper than the length of my arm, for I could just barely reach to the shutters. As I was doing this I put the lamp down on the sill and moved my head up to undo a bolt on the shutter. Then I saw, on a huge stone slab, some sort of writing.

'Look!' I screamed, 'Look what I've found!'

As more lanterns were brought, we saw very clearly a stone with inscriptions all the way down. And our Spanish friend said, 'Aline, these are Latin inscriptions. I have seen them before. It looks like a Roman tombstone.'

We found others as we went on. How strange, I thought, one upside down in the window, one in the floor, another in a wall— could that mean that bodies are buried here?

On we went through this long, high building of stone, which now, we could see, had once been a large rectangular building with a patio in the centre. Again we went upstairs, by the same outside steps, to another enormous room which looked like a chapel. At one end was a balcony with stairs leading up to it.

'This was once the watch tower of the house,' explained Juan, 'but now we store seed here.'

Luis, who always tends to make sense while I go off on tangents, suddenly asked, 'Juan, why is it that we had to come out to the patio to come up to this floor. Why is there no stairway inside the house from the first to the second floor?'

'This *palacio* is very strange, Señor Conde. Everything about it is strange.'

With that, Luis began tapping on the walls. 'But Juan, it is not

25

possible that there is no inside staircase. It must be hidden somewhere in the building. But why would anyone have blocked it up? Where could it be?'

By now we had already inspected some fourteen or fifteen stone rooms and the emotion and excitement of the day had taken its toll. We were dead tired and decided it was time to turn in. The servants had prepared four rooms for us, in various parts of the house.

'Don't think for one minute I'm going to sleep so far away from the rest of you in this weird place,' said Annabella. 'I have never been so terrified in my life.'

So Annabella's bed was moved into the room with Luis and me. But our Spanish friend also demurred at sleeping in the downstairs room marked for him.

'It is not that I am afraid, of course,' he said. 'But I think I would just as soon not sleep down there. Who knows what one might find.'

Our Brazilian guests invited him into their room, she saying, 'Yes, yes, of course we understand, and who knows, there might be ghosts here.'

'Ghosts,' I asked delighted. 'Juan, are there any ghosts in Pascualete?'

I was surprised to see an expression of fear come into his eyes. 'Oh, Señora Condesa, nothing like that has ever happened here, *Gracias a Dios*. Oh, no, there are no ghosts at Pascualete,' he said nervously, and then with his second and small finger made the classic sign of the devil's horns and touched wood.

The other servants were scurrying to rearrange the beds, somewhat shocked by our unorthodox sleeping arrangements. On the country beds were high straw mattresses which, I suppose to provide more luxurious comfort than usual, had been stuffed over three feet high. Annabella's bed was particularly high and in order to get her into it, Luis and our Brazilian friend had to take her by the feet and head and swing her up and she disappeared into the deep straw.

And so, finally, we slept.

Journey into the Unknown

The next morning we reassembled in the room where we had dined and found Maria on her knees preparing coffee, toast and eggs. We were greeted with curtsies and bright smiles and invited to supervise the preparation of our soft-boiled eggs as they bubbled away in pots on the open fire before us.

Hurriedly we finished our breakfast, impatient to get out into the fresh, sun-drenched countryside which we glimpsed through the single small balcony window.

When we descended the winding stone stairs to the ground floor and retraced our wanderings of the night before we discovered that the darkness concealed great vaulted ceilings and enormous Romanesque doorways leading from one room to another.

We emerged into the sunlit patio and saw it was enclosed on three sides by ancient cowsheds of the same stone as the long rectangular palace which formed its fourth side.

'Look,' said Luis, as he pushed open a half-shattered wooden door leading into one of the cowsheds. Amazed, we peered down a seemingly endless *cañon* arch which formed an elegant ceiling for the home of about a hundred cows. On either side were carved stone feed troughs worn with many centuries of use.

A motley collection of mules, *burros* and work horses were being saddled in the patio, and we were graciously offered mounts to proceed on our investigation of the property. We wound our way down through the open wheatfields and rolling groves of evergreen oaks to the river about four kilometres distant.

Suddenly Luis shouted, 'Primitivo, ride back to the house quickly and bring me my shotgun from the car.' I knew he was excited and amazed at the abundance of partridge, hare and other game.

Every now and then we saw clustered on the little hill-tops round straw mounds which upon closer inspection proved to be the homes of shepherds who cared for the flocks of sheep in that area. We finally arrived at a high cliff which looked down into a deep and perilous gorge where the rushing waters of a small river swirled against the steep stone walls.

27

The Discovery of Pascualete

And so, with one enchanting discovery after another, the day passed. All the way back to Madrid I thought of the house, with its timeless atmosphere, its peace and tranquillity, its voice from the past waiting to reveal so much to me. That house, I knew would be something decisive in my life.

3

Renovating the 'Palacio'

FOR ONE REASON or another, I did not return to Pascualete until a little over a year later. I was almost seven months pregnant and anxious to get away from the eyes of everyone, so I took the two children to spend a few weeks in Estremadura. This time Luis gave all assistance to the plan but was unable to accompany me.

It was January and unusually cold. Three times we lost our way in the darkness on the cowpath leading to the house. As we finally passed through the entrance arch we heard the wind hissing and wailing round the eaves of the stone building and bits of straw and dust whirled in the air before our headlights. The storm must have completely blotted out the sound of our arrival because not a person nor an animal was in sight.

The baby stirred in the old nurse's arms and started to cry. Two-year old Alvaro was asleep in my lap and as I leaned over impatiently in front of the chauffeur to blow the horn, Alvaro also awakened and cried.

I gave Alvaro to the nurse and stumbled out of the car to knock on the big solid wooden door of the guard's house. This was a long thin building squeezed up against one corner of the rectangular patio. I hurt my knuckles on the rough iron nail heads covering its surface and I was choking in the litter of dust and stray bits that were blowing about my head, when the upper half of the door swung open abruptly and Primitivo's face appeared, lined and darker than ever in the shadows. His black eyes stared at me bewildered.

'But we had no word the Señora Condesa was coming. This is terrible! Nothing is prepared!'

The Discovery of Pascualete

'Didn't you receive the message the Señor Conde sent a week ago?' I asked.

By now Maria had appeared carrying an assortment of long rusty iron keys. She was fully dressed and much more in command of the situation than her husband. Her expressionless face showed no sign of concern. Only her voice revealed that she was upset and hurried. She bowed ceremoniously, taking my hand, and suggested I keep the children in the car until candles had been lit and a fire started.

After a short interval Maria descended to inform us that we could enter and led us up the stairs into the house. I looked about me. Eight new rush-bottomed chairs were piled in a corner and next to them some rough-hewn bars which proved to be two dismantled beds. Luis had told me that there would be plenty of furniture, for he had ordered it after our first visit to the *finca*. And this was it. Not one other thing was in any of the rooms we were to occupy.

Maria understood my face of despair.

'Now, now, the Señora Condesa must not fret. I have an excellent crib for the baby. My Augustina is six years old now and too big for it anyway. Also my *mesa camilla* takes up too much room in my little house.'

'But the dishes, Maria, and the sheets—there seemed to be so many things here the last time I came.'

'Well, those things belonged to the wife of the *arrendatario* and to me. We wanted the Señores Condes to be comfortable. The house has never had any furniture or belongings in our time nor in the time of Primitivo's father either. But there is no cause for worry. In ten minutes the Señora Condesa will have all that is necessary.'

And she was right. Within no time the beds were up, fresh straw mattresses were prepared with clean-smelling sheets and warm wool blankets. Luisito was already in Tina's crib in the next room and complaining bitterly, but Alvaro was happy again running around among all the busy people. Suddenly I heard him stumble and shriek. Rushing to pick him up, I found his mouth was bleeding profusely. He had broken his front tooth right in half—one of the few teeth he had.

What a disaster this trip has been, I thought, as I finally got into bed. Why did I bring the children to this isolated place? What if they get sick and no doctor for miles? Really, why had Luis let me come?

But things are never so bad in the light of day, and the next morning I cheered up as I launched various projects for making Pascualete habitable again.

As we huddled round the table eating breakfast in our over-coats, I realized the first thing I had to do was put glass in the windows, for once the shutters were opened to let in the daylight, they also let in the cold January wind. I summoned Juan, who had been waiting outside in the patio.

'Juan, I have a great deal of work I want done in this house and I need many workers.'

'We are at the disposal of the Señora Condesa,' he said and then disappeared a moment and returned with three men whom he introduced as his brothers.

As the four men stood at attention I felt like a drill sergeant.

'The first thing we must do is put glass in the windows,' I said emphatically.

They seemed to find this a little strange. 'But Señora Condesa, we have to send to Trujillo for the glass, and I do not know if there is anyone around here who knows how to cut it. Perhaps the carpenter in Santa Marta would know how to do it,' Juan added a bit dubiously.

This was the first time that I realized there was a village near by called Santa Marta, and it brought to my mind that Luis' grandfather, the Conde de Torre Arias, also had had the title of Marqués de Santa Marta.

'I must send a man right away, for it will take at least two hours to bring the carpenter here,' he added.

'But, Juan, if the village is close by, why on earth will it take so long?'

'The Señora Condesa does not realize that there is only a

The Discovery of Pascualete

cowpath to Santa Marta. We will send someone by the fastest horse we have, but even so two, maybe even three hours is the best we can hope for. I do not dare to send the Señora Condesa's nice car for fear it would be destroyed!'

And Juan disappeared, presumably to dispatch a man to Santa Marta, so I addressed myself to the next one.

'Now I need at least four more chairs and two beds,' and I went ahead explaining my measurements. The second brother grinned happily at me and continued grinning and nodding his head.

Finally another brother, José, said 'I am sorry, Señora Condesa, but Alberto does not hear very well.'

It was apparent that Alberto not only didn't hear well but didn't hear at all. However, José reassured me about the furniture.

'It will be very easy to make all the furniture the Señora Condesa wants,' he said. '*Gracias a Dios*, Pascualete does not lack trees and we have several dead ones now that we can use.' Then he disappeared.

To the fourth brother I said, 'Of course, we shall need mattresses . . . ' and I stopped. He, too, grinned foolishly, and I wondered if deafness ran in the family. But not at all. When he finally opened his mouth to speak, he was so voluble I could hardly stop him.

'Oh, Señora Condesa, if we cannot make mattresses here then there is no place in the world that can make mattresses. Here in Estremadura we have the finest wool from the Merino sheep— and the sheep at Pascualete are the best of all the Merinos. I personally will cut the wool with my own hands, I will weigh it with my own hands and then my women will wash it . . .'

'Marvellous, marvellous.' I finally cut off this eulogy and he left. So there I was with Alberto, and not knowing what to do, I began making signs of a hammer and nails, and beaming with comprehension, he left me in the middle of a sentence and off he went.

From this day on I discovered I loved giving orders, and every morning thereafter the four brothers would appear, hats in hand, waiting for their daily instructions.

Renovating the 'Palacio'

Afterwards, I would go down to the patio, and from the landing of the steps I could watch the frenzy of activity—painting, carpentry, cutting wood, bringing water—for the entire life of Pascualete was centred in that patio. It was always filled with people and animals and from my vantage point I could see everything that was going on.

One of the things that amused me most was the morning ritual of Isidora, the fat, middle-aged wife of one of the cowherds. Her first act was to comb her long dark hair, so matted with grease that the filthy broken-toothed comb could barely get through it. She combed slowly and deliberately, dipping the ugly black comb every few moments into a basin of water in her lap. After five minutes of this she took her two able hands and slid her hair back sleekly into position, gripping the long tail and twisting it at the nape of her neck into a neat, artistic little knot.

Her beauty treatment for the day being over, Isidora bounced up from her low rush-bottomed chair, tossed the contents of the white pan over the patio wall and went into her stone house adjoining the cow stalls, emerging again with two enormous clay water jugs. At the well just outside the patio she filled both jugs, and in one smooth movement swung the first clay jug on to the top of her head and then, holding her shoulders, neck and head very stiffly, reached down and grabbed the other jug which she placed on her well-padded hip. She walked majestically back to her little door and, if I happened to be watching, she made it a point to turn her head sideways now and then so that I might see with what ease she carried her burden.

In a few minutes she again emerged, this time with a Singer sewing machine, vintage 1910, which she set up in the same sunny corner outside her door. Always singing some tuneless song, she pumped the pedal with vigour and moved quantities of old clothes back and forth under the needle.

Seeing the sewing machine that first day, I realized I had found an invaluable aid in my redecorating schemes. I walked across the patio to her.

The Discovery of Pascualete

'Isidora, do you suppose you could help me make the curtains for the house?' I asked.

Her round face beamed with pleasure. 'Ah, Señora Condesita, we country women take great pride in our sewing. It will be a privilege to help the Señora Condesita and we can even weave the material, if she would like.'

From then on I discovered the delights of a morning conversation with Isidora. She always had a juicy or dramatic bit saved for me, generally a catastrophe of one sort or another. One day it was how her son had caught his hands while fixing the spokes of a cartwheel; another day, her sister-in-law's child had fallen down the well. And if I mentioned any ailment, she was quick to prescribe all sorts of miraculous herbs which she produced wrapped in filthy paper parcels.

Making my usual rounds one morning I noticed something new in Isidora's appearance—a pair of black-rimmed spectacles rested precariously on the tip of her nose.

'Ah, I can see the Señora Condesita is admiring my new spectacles,' she said smugly.

As I came closer I could see that a dirty cord encircled her head and held the contraption in place.

'New!' I replied. 'Isidora, I have never seen anything so old in my life. Where did you get them?'

'The barber in Santa Marta sold them to me for $3.50. They belonged to his mother who now rests in peace.'

As Isidora spoke she removed the spectacles and turned them over admiringly in her hands for a few moments and then ceremoniously, exactly as one dons a hat, she put them back in position.

'At least the Señora Condesita must admit they give one a great air of importance. No one else in Pascualete has ever owned spectacles before and they say that they are very helpful in threading small needles.'

A few days after I had marshalled my army of workers, I decided to go into Trujillo to telephone Luis and I told Juan to inform the chauffeur we would leave immediately.

Isidora and her new spectacles

Looking into
the patio
of the house
from the well

Renovating the 'Palacio'

'Oh, no, no,' said Juan shaking his head, 'the Señora Condesa cannot hope to speak with Madrid today. Why it is already noon.'

'Juan, I have all the afternoon,' I reminded him.

'But to make a telephone call to Madrid, the Señora Condesa must rise at six in the morning and drive to Trujillo at once in time to place the call before nine o'clock. Even then it might take all day to get through to the Señor Conde.'

'Oh dear,' I cried, 'and I was so anxious to talk at once to the Señor Conde so he might send some furniture and foodstuffs down by truck. I had hoped to have these things by tomorrow night.'

But again Juan was shaking his head sadly and patiently and saying, 'No, no.'

'Now, what's the matter Juan?'

'Perhaps the Señora Condesa does not realize that a truck cannot possibly come on the cowpath to Pascualete. Of course, I will be glad to send out a cart and team of oxen to bring whatever the Señora Condesa wants. But we must make these plans ahead of time so that the oxen can leave at four o'clock in the morning. It takes five hours to get to Trujillo where they will meet the truck, then they must load everything and then five hours back. *Sí, sí,* it requires time.'

Everything, I soon realized, required infinite amounts of time, but despite these frustrations, I was happy and so wrapped up in my work that I almost managed to forget I was pregnant.

But my poor old nurse, or *ama,* as the children called her, was miserable. The fat, lovable creature grumbled incessantly.

'Never, not even in my native village, have I ever lived in such surroundings,' she would mutter under her breath. 'Only the poorest people live like this, with no heat, no electricity, no water. It is not that I object to being in the country, but people of quality have country houses in keeping with their station in life. In my last position I lived like a queen, and here I am living like an animal.'

Alas, I did not take her too seriously, until one evening in the middle of dinner I heard a frightful racket on the stone steps outside. I ran to the door and was horrified to see our dear old *ama*—all two hundred pounds of her—sprawled out at the bottom of the steps. Guided only by the uncertain glimmer of a candle, *ama* had missed her step and fallen the entire length of the stairs, bumping her head on each step. I still do not understand how she survived, but apart from a very bloody wound on her forehead, she seemed all right and quite indignant, and we were obliged to send her back to Madrid and civilization on the first bus.

However, nothing could discourage me now. I had drawn up something resembling a floor plan to guide me in my renovations. The large central room downstairs, where we first saw the *escudo*, was the obvious choice for the main salon or hall. And all the long series of rooms on either side I wanted to make into bedrooms, bathrooms and small sitting-rooms. The chapel-like room upstairs was to be the dining-room, and I hoped to continue with the huge fireplace serving as a kitchen.

I also realized that this room could not have been a chapel, as I had originally thought, for right on the patio was a little church with its belfry and the same *escudo* of the five roses over the doorway. This building had long since ceased to be used for religious purposes, even though it still had a lovely marble altar. The black-scarred walls revealed that it had probably been used for smoking hams. I made a mental note that we would one day restore the church.

But for the moment I had to concern myself with a basic necessity to my American way of thinking—a bathroom. I could not go on with this system of bringing all our water up from the well and chamber pots under the beds.

When I first broached the subject with Juan I could see he had no idea what I meant. Finally, I had to use the more vulgar word for toilet.

'Now I understand,' he said, a bit embarrassed. 'In our houses we do not have these modern innovations. We do not find them very necessary. Of course, I have heard that such apparatuses are used and I realize that perhaps a great lady such as the Señora

Condesa might want one. I know they sell them in Trujillo, as I have seen them there. Of course, we shall have to send a team of oxen to fetch this machine, but as all the carts are out on missions for the Señora Condesa, it might be several days before this can be done.'

I also told Juan to order me several hundred tiles in different designs such as I had seen around the *finca* and that I knew were made in Santa Marta. I wanted to make the tub and sink out of tiles so as not to detract from the ancient character of the house.

'Do you know of a plumber, Juan?'

'What exactly does a plumber do, Señora Condesa?'

I explained that he puts tubes and pipes together so that water will flow into these machines and Juan said, 'Well, I do not know of anyone who calls himself a plumber, but I do not see why a good bricklayer could not do the work as well.'

And so, I became the plumbing engineer, with the bricklayer to carry out my ideas. We ordered a big water tank from Trujillo and put it on the roof and then with much difficulty we bored holes through the stone walls for the connecting pipes. One day, while having lunch in front of the fireplace, it occurred to me that I also could have HOT water by putting still another tank in the wall of the chimney and connecting it with a pipe to the bathroom.

The workmen lent themselves to the creation of a bathroom with great enthusiasm, even though they were not quite certain what might result. The tub was a truly grand affair, large and square, faced with the brilliantly coloured tiles and the tile basin rested on two cement legs, wonderfully crooked.

With great pride, the workmen came to the patio one day and announced, 'The "*salon de aguas*" (hall of waters) of the Señora Condesa is now finished and awaiting her approval.'

They looked so pleased while I investigated the details of this unusual room. But there was one slight omission. The basin, a work of art with blue and yellow tiles forming intricate designs, had no hole for drainage. I explained to them that I wanted a basin that drained.

The Discovery of Pascualete

'Oh, the needs of the Señora Condesa will be taken care of immediately. Nothing is simpler!'

I went on about my work and was startled when a few minutes later I was called up to view the basin which now drained. Amazed that these simple workmen had managed to install and connect the necessary pipe for the drainage so quickly, I rushed up. There I viewed the basin which drained. They had merely cut a small hole in the centre and had placed below on the floor an old bucket.

The first bath was a memorable event. Heating the water in the new tank did not take long but filling the enormous tub took about forty-five minutes. And by the time the tank was empty, the tub was barely covered. Maria had made a fire in the chimney and was watching dubiously. Despite the fire, the stone floor and walls and high ceilings remained chilly, and I was shivering when I got into the tub. About one inch of my body was covered by the hot water which we had taken such trouble to install and which by now was rapidly cooling off. I could see Maria was thinking she would stick to her country practice of a sponge bath once a year.

'That is certainly the most foolish and hazardous undertaking I have ever seen,' she said. 'If the Señora Condesa does not take her death of cold it will be nothing short of a miracle!'

Now I turned my attention to the large downstairs room which was to be the salon. It seemed strange that a room so large had no window, especially as I had noticed a window from the outside of the house in a part of the wall that corresponded to the main room. I called several workmen together and by tapping around we discovered one of the inner walls to be hollow.

'Tear this wall down,' I said and as the startled men began to work, the wall yielded rapidly to their pick-axes. Soon the window and a whole new alcove appeared amidst the debris. I had never realized until that moment the fascination of seeing a wall fall revealing a whole new horizon.

Delighted with this quick success, I then remembered Luis' concern during our first trip that Pascualete had no interior staircase.

Renovating the 'Palacio'

'Juan, there must be a staircase in this room as well. This is the logical place for it.'

So we tapped some more and it was decided that perhaps one small part of another wall might be false and the pickaxes set to work again. I was terrified my luck would not hold, but this wall gave way as quickly as the other and disclosed, to our amazement, a tunnel-like stairway leading to the upper floor.

Every day now I was expecting Luis' arrival and I was anxious to have the place completely transformed before he came. I had written him nothing, hoping to surprise him.

My next project was making a dining-room table. We needed a particularly large tree and found an old black poplar which had fallen in a storm some years ago. A specialist from La Cumbre, a near-by village, was summoned to come and haul it away and he promised that my measurements of fifteen feet by three feet would be met. The table was returned in three long planks drawn by a cart and four oxen and set up in the dining-room with much banging and ceremony.

'If I say so myself,' said the carpenter, 'this is truly a magnificent table, worthy of a house of the Señores Condes and may I add that I hope that the great-grandchildren of the Señores Condes will one day be enjoying this marvellous table.'

I hate to spoil my story so soon, but six months later our table had warped and now the plates on one side have a tendency to run away, while on the other side they fall into one's lap. However, I still hope the carpenter's prophecy comes true.

Whenever I was not working—and especially in the evenings after the sunset—I often took this opportunity to get to know these wonderful, simple people who now filled my life. I got in the habit of visiting Isidora every evening when her three sons returned from their work in the fields and when her husband Paco had finally tucked away and fed the last cow in his shed.

I would find the four men seated in front of a tiny fire which she made on the stone floor in one of the two rooms they inhabited. This fire consisted of a few twigs and light branches leaning against the wall, also of stone. There was no chimney,

The Discovery of Pascualete

and sometimes the smoke was so thick I could not stay very long, but at other times the fire burned brightly and the smoke seemed to disappear as if by magic.

A large double bed almost filled the room and the ceiling was covered with strings of Spanish sausages and bright red tomatoes which glistened in the light of the small fire. (I was amazed to learn that tomatoes and grapes might be kept for many months by stringing them up in a room with good air and ventilation.)

Just outside the door two long files of cows were tied in their open stalls, loudly munching the straw in the old stone troughs. A couple of donkeys at the further end now and then gave a kick to one of the cows and then the cowherd would grab an oil lantern from the wall and walk up the path between the two lines of cows, his worn leather chaps swish-swashing cosily. He scolded the animals for their misbehaviour, as if they were his children:

'Petra, Petra, move over and give the poor old *burro* room to lie down. He has carried many sacks of logs today and he deserves to sleep as well as you. If you are a good girl I will give you an extra handful of straw in the morning. You should be ashamed of yourself for always causing a fuss with your old friend.'

This soft-hearted old man was squat, with a square bewhiskered face and a thatch of wiry grey hair held down by a grubby old felt hat. I noticed that the men at Pascualete always wore a hat indoors, as well as outside. The only time any of them removed their hats was when they came to talk to me. Strangely enough they seemed to lose all their self-assurance when they had their hats off.

Once when I remarked to Juan about his affection for his hat, he told me that during the Civil War he was captured by the 'Reds' and led into a near-by village to appear before the judge. His hands were tied behind his back and the first thing the judge barked out was:

'When in the presence of a Judge your hat is supposed to be removed! Why do all you country people think you can go everywhere with a hat on?'

Renovating the 'Palacio'

Juan said he had a good answer for that one, which he told me in his chuckling slow drawl. 'Well, if you would just untie my hands, I might be able to do something about the hat!' 'They were mean fellows,' he went on to say, 'but they did not get the better of me. I left my hat on all the time!'

One day, as I was on a ladder trying to nail some curtains over the window, Maria appeared.

'Pedro, the young shepherd is outside,' she informed me, 'and he says he has an urgent matter to discuss with the Señora Condesa.'

A few minutes later a clean-cut blond young man with a red face bowed his way into the room. He looked nervous and troubled.

'If the Señora Condesa will forgive me for troubling her, I wanted to report that last night our donkey was stolen. And I wondered if the Señora Condesa might do us the favour of watching the animals on the road to Trujillo, in case she might be able to recognize our poor old Clementina.'

'But Pedro, how would I ever recognize your donkey from any other? They all look alike to me.'

'Oh, anyone could recognize Clementina. She has the softest silver grey coat of any *burra* in Estremadura and certainly her brown eyes are much more expressive than those shabby-looking donkeys that Juan and Primitivo keep out in the paddock. And she was so gentle with all the children. They used to love to watch her try to flick the flies off her nose with her long pointed ears.'

'Have you any idea what could have happened?'

'We looked for her footprints and they seemed to go in the direction of Trujillo.'

'Must be those damned thieving gipsies,' interjected Primitivo, who had overheard the conversation. 'Not the first time they have stolen animals from Pascualete.'

Pedro turned to me again and went on speaking. 'It is a great loss to us. Not only do we love her very much but all our savings are put in that *burra*. Each year she provided us with a foal which

41

would bring sometimes as much as 600 pesetas in the fair in Trujillo and she herself was worth fully 3,000 pesetas.'

I promised to advise the police in Trujillo and to keep my eyes open on the way in.

The next morning as we arrived at the macadam road to Trujillo I saw a mountain of twigs walking towards me. The little donkey underneath was completely invisible and only his dainty black feet proved that he was there at all. He walked as primly as a lady in her highest heeled shoes and not even the noisy Ford interrupted his dreams as he pranced along his way. I was all for making the tired wizened farmer who walked by his side remove the last twig in order to determine whether or not this could be Pedro's lost *burra*, but Primitivo seemed to know immediately that it was not the animal we were looking for.

'How can you recognize a donkey from its feet?' I demanded.

'Clementina steps much more gracefully and anyhow she is larger,' Primitivo replied.

Every few moments we passed donkeys on our way but each time Primitivo shook his head sadly.

Alas, the lost Clementina was never found and we assumed that the gipsies in their cunning way got off scot free once again.

During those early days at Pascualete, I would have been lost without Pepe, our chauffeur. He was tall and dark, with a handsome face and pleasant manner and when he first came to work for us it quickly became evident that his abilities far surpassed those of any normal chauffeur. We learned that in his previous jobs he had been alternately a cook, a cabinet maker, painter and plumber. All this was particularly extraordinary since Pepe was only twenty-two.

At Pascualete he was all over the place. He decided that Maria's primitive cooking was not good enough for me or the children and improvised the most exotic dishes over the difficult open fire. Being something of an actor, he fashioned himself a chef's hat and tied a napkin round his neck to give the proper effect while cooking.

Pepe had only one fault—his Don Juan attitude with women.

A view
of a corner
of the house
taken from
the main patio

Water cart
just outside
one of the walls
of the patio

Renovating the 'Palacio'

At the farm three or four giggling, blushing country girls followed him wherever he went. And when I reprimanded him, he answered with feigned innocence, 'What can I do if women plague me?'

However, despite this failing, Pepe was indispensable as carpenter, cook and baby's nurse and could ill afford the time it took to drive the car.

I used to keep some of the extra workmen from Santa Marta so late at night trying to finish that often I had Pepe drive them home to save the hour's walk. But one evening Pepe was so busy I decided to take on the job. The path to Santa Marta was far worse than the one to the main road, and I was quite relieved when the little town finally came into view. A few pale street oil lights flickered over the group of low, dark buildings and I could barely make out the picturesque grey arched doorway of what I was proudly told was the church.

A family of fat pigs got in our way and we could go no further. Before I could even turn the car round, mothers and wives and children began to swarm about us. One of the steady helpers at Pascualete, *El Barbero*, so called because he was also the town barber, brought his buxom wife to be introduced.

'Would the Señora Condesa kindly honour our humble home?' she said as she indicated a small doorway at the side of the road. I expected a thoroughly miserable scene of dirt and disorder and I was amazed to find a spotlessly clean little room whose red and white tiled floor sparkled in the rays of the family fire. Several copper pots gleamed decoratively on the whitewashed wall above the hearth and a small *mesa camilla* with two chairs occupied the centre of the room. Near the hearth were several little three-legged stools and in a far corner three tiny children were sitting on the floor playing.

'Please take a seat,' she said. 'Would the Señora Condesa try my home-cured ham and a glass of wine?' she asked as she sliced some ample portions. I realized that *El Barbero*'s wife was offering me the food for herself and her family for several days, but there was no way to refuse.

The Discovery of Pascualete

Later, as I returned to Pascualete, a terrible storm broke out, which kept on for days. On the fourth night—I remember it was February 10—I heard a knock on the door.

'Just a minute,' I called as I jumped up and quickly threw on my dressing gown. It was Juan and his brother José standing side by side, twisting their hats in their hands and looking very uncomfortable.

'What is the matter?' I asked.

Juan began, then his brother José put in a few words, then he stopped helplessly and Juan with great difficulty and embarassment blurted out:

'Señora Condesa, the water is rising so fast and the dirt lanes are so filled with mud that if the Señora Condesa does not leave immediately this same night, she might not be able to leave for ten days.'

When I did not look particularly upset by that, Juan haltingly went on to explain that they were not very adept at helping ladies to give birth and a hospital in Madrid might be more comfortable. And considering that I certainly must be on the point of producing a child, they advised me to leave that very night.

I awakened the children and dressed them and with great reluctance left early in the morning, with the aid of a pair of oxen who had to pull us through the first two mud ponds. My only thought was to dispatch with this child as quickly as possible and return to my work at Pascualete.

4

Pillete, the delightful Rascal of Trujillo

AFTER GIVING BIRTH to Miguel, my visits to Pascualete were as frequent as possible and I had to spend more and more time in Trujillo on buying expeditions. But I never seemed to know where to shop for the various things we needed. Materials and wool, pots and pans, nails, paint, wire—each was sold in a different store hidden away in one of those twisted streets. But the day I met Pillete my life changed considerably.

Pepe, the chauffeur, had driven me into Trujillo that day, and we had stopped at the two petrol pumps hoping to fill our tank, but the attendants told us there was not a drop of petrol in the Trujillo area. Their pumps had been dry for ten days.

'Pepe, we haven't enough petrol to get back to Pascualete,' I pointed out, as we drove through one of the four large archways leading into the main plaza. 'And look at these two cars here in the plaza. They must have got some petrol somewhere.'

It was a grey, rainy day and the main square of Trujillo was deserted except for two old jalopies, more practical than one might think, for they were the best cars to take the bumps and ruts of the primitive country roads.

'Señora Condesa, I think I know the only man in Trujillo who could help us,' he said. 'I am afraid to ask him myself. I am not important enough for him to do such a big favour for me, but if I introduce the Señora Condesa to him, I am sure he would help us.'

'Who is this man?' I asked.

'His name is Pillete and he owns the bar over there,' said Pepe, pointing.

I looked around the arcaded plaza where he indicated and saw a sign 'Bar Imperio' written across a building which was once a palace—all the buildings facing the plaza were once palaces but now the lower stories had been converted into stores and business establishments, with living quarters up above.

As we approached the Bar Imperio, I could see that there was a place for an awning and that probably in the summer it was easily converted into a sidewalk café. But now everyone was huddled inside, and as we entered I smelled the pleasant scent of coffee mingled with the heavy bitter smoke of black tobacco.

Swarms of men were playing cards at the black marble-topped, iron-legged tables while onlookers were drinking and talking. At the far end a young boy in a white coat stood at a long white marble counter serving drinks to a line of weather-beaten farmers.

The men all had their hats on, but their country canes were propped neatly against a column in the centre of the room and their big black boots made loud noises on the tile floors as they shifted their feet restlessly.

As Pepe looked around searching for the proprietor, I saw a short, fat little man with dark skin, cheerful small black eyes and a bulbous nose waddle towards us.

'*Buenos dias*, Pepe,' he said, 'What can I do for you today?'

'I want to present you to the Señora Condesa,' said Pepe. And Pillete beamed at me, showing a prominent gold tooth as he smiled. He wore a little black beret perched over his sparse greying hair and there was a stubble of beard on his ample cheeks. He rubbed his hands vigorously on his trousers before shaking my hand.

'This is a great pleasure, Señora Condesa,' he said as he bowed. 'We all know about the wonderful things the Señora Condesa is doing at Pascualete. What can we do to serve her? My wife and my five sons are at her disposal.'

With that he snapped his fingers imperiously at the young white-coated men whom I had observed working like demons, and they all stopped in their tracks and came running at his command.

From a back room appeared his wife, Candida, who was a feminine replica of Pillete. She too was short and plump, and she

The entrance arch at Pascualete through
which is seen the façade of the chapel

Pillete

had the same little black eyes, the same walk, the same round pleasant face and even the same gold tooth!

'Yes, there really is something you can do for me,' I explained to Pillete, after the amenities were over, and I told him about the petrol.

'Well, Señora Condesa, I am not rich enough to have a car myself, but I have many friends who have cars and petrol. In fact, just over there in the corner is a man who might be able to help us—and knowing that it is for the Señora Condesa, I am sure he will find you all the petrol you need.'

With that problem all but solved, Candida warmly invited me to sit down and have a cup of coffee, while Pillete went off to negotiate for my petrol. Delighted, I sat down, but his wife remained standing.

'Please, Candida, do sit down with me. Perhaps you could give me some suggestions about where I might find some of these things on my shopping list.'

I needed blankets, towels, material for curtains, some bed-springs, butter, vegetables . . .

'This is a very discouraging list,' I added, as I finished reading it off.

'No, no, Señora Condesa, everything is very simple. You sit here and relax and I will send my sons to buy everything for you.

'Juan,' she cried, 'go at once to Hernando's and bring several blankets for the Señora Condesa to inspect. Be sure they give you a good price and new ones, not last year's which have been sitting around collecting dampness and bugs.' And in an aside to me she added, 'I know that the store the Señora Condesa has been using for her dry goods is very unreliable.'

'And you,' as she beckoned to another son, 'tell Don Alfredo to send us a dozen of his best towels. And stop by the butter shop, be sure it is the freshest butter she has.'

The boys disappeared in all different directions, and this accomplished, Candida said to me, 'Perhaps the Señora Condesa would like to use our telephone. We have one of the few telephones in Trujillo,' she added with pride. 'And we have noticed that the Señora Condesa comes often to the telephone company to call to Madrid, and that many times she waits all day. Perhaps she would be more comfortable placing her calls here.'

I was amused to realize that I had been so carefully observed during my previous visits, and that all my movements had been duly noted and discussed.

'Thank you so much,' I said, 'but now it is a little late to place the call.'

'Perhaps not, Señora Condesa. My son's *novia* is the telephone operator and perhaps he can help you get it through more quickly.'

So Juan placed my call to Madrid, and within an hour I was speaking with Luis! Now I realized what Pepe meant when he described Pillete as the most important and influential man in Trujillo.

From then on the corner table at the Bar Imperio became my office, and it became sheer necessity for me, in order to do my shopping, to consult with Pillete and Candida while their five sons attended to my complicated errands. They never allowed me to pay for one cup of coffee nor would any of the sons ever accept a tip for their troubles.

Gradually, I made friends with many of the customers of the bar, most of whom were farmers from the neighbouring country-side. There was no problem which could not be solved by a visit to Pillete's establishment, and if, for some reason, he could not handle it, one of my new-found friends was bound to come up with an answer.

I especially liked coming to town on Thursdays, the day of the weekly fair, when the Bar Imperio became the meeting place for hundreds of smocked and cane-carrying farmers. At about eleven-thirty in the morning, with loud cries and gesticulations, they proceeded to buy and sell sheep, pigs and fodder. It was a real Stock Exchange, as active, and certainly as colourful as any I have seen in Wall Street or Madrid.

With Pillete at my side, all sorts of doors were opened for me. This energetic, clever man also owned an ice factory and was a

Pillete, the delightful Rascal of Trujillo

skilful carpenter as well. He had a cabinet maker's business which he claimed produced the finest furniture in Estremadura. In business he was shrewd and although no one could ever fool him, he was popular with the entire town and was known as an honest, good, reliable man. The nuns and priests especially adored him because he sent them food and provisions at his own expense during the Spanish Civil War.

One day, while sitting at my table in the Bar Imperio with one of my new friends, I asked why there were so few women in Trujillo and none in the bar. He graciously offered me the ingredients for rolling a cigarette, and then with what seemed to me a shy glance at my blue jeans, he answered, 'It is not the custom of the "ladies" of Trujillo to go to bars. Their days are spent in their homes, taking care of children.'

My pride in having become 'one of the boys' was shattered. The black tobacco in the rolled cigarette tasted still more bitter; and my jeans, in which I thought I cut a neat figure, suddenly seemed indecent. I realized that of course, a Spanish woman, whatever her age or figure, would never wear pants in a public place. After that I found that a divided skirt was almost as practical and although I continued my visits to the Bar, I restricted the use of pants to the *finca* only.

Now that I considered myself a native of Estremadura, it was especially annoying always to find masses of children following me from store to store. They even followed me in Caceres, a city almost ten times larger than Trujillo and far more cosmopolitan, where I often went to do my more complicated shopping. One day I turned around quickly and grabbed one of the little boys who had been on my trail for the past two hours.

'Tell me, little one, why are you following me? Am I so different from all the other ladies in the street?' I asked.

I had dressed very carefully in a dark suit and low walking shoes and considered my costume very discreet. The child's big brown eyes, shining out of his pale little face, became round with amazement.

'But Señora, you are wearing a hat.'

49

The Discovery of Pascualete

So, it was my old shooting hat which gave me away! After that, I tried these expeditions without a hat, but it was no use. Then I remembered how strange and different out-of-towners always looked to us in Pearl River. It did not have to be a hat or anything in particular. We just knew.

I often threatened Pillete as he walked with me through the streets of Trujillo shooing off children, village idlers and even a few stray cats and dogs. 'One day I'm going to appear here in my *guardesa*'s black city-going dress and wrap up my head in her old black scarf. Then maybe no one will notice me.'

With that Pillete let out his deep guttural laugh—so contagious that everyone around has to laugh with him. With me especially, Pillete always seemed to be laughing because for some unknown reason he found everything I said funny.

From the first day I met Pillete, I was never permitted to walk alone in Trujillo again. Pillete became my shadow, even carrying my packages for me, despite the fact that in Spain a man considers this degrading.

Even though they never said anything, I suppose Pillete and his family wondered when the Conde de Quintanilla would appear on the scene.

Actually, Luis was anxious to come. From the first trip, he had seen that Pascualete was rich with partridge and other birds and especially wanted to try the shooting. Also, his entire family, by now, was curious about my activities in Estremadura. But I made him promise not to come until I had everything arranged. Finally, when the first renovations were completed I was honoured by a visit from Luis and his father.

They were enchanted with everything I had done and Luis fell in love with Pascualete that week-end. From that moment on my struggles to arrange the house were completely shared by him. However, as he always drove directly to the *finca* I never had a chance to introduce Luis to Pillete and my circle of friends at the Bar Imperio. I was worried, too, that Luis might not approve of my somewhat rough-looking friends, as Spanish husbands are apt to put limitations on a wife's activities and tastes.

Pillete, the delightful Rascal of Trujillo

One week-end I was expecting Luis in time for lunch, but he did not arrive. As hour after hour went by I became desperate, imagining all sorts of terrible accidents, when at last I heard his car.

'What on earth happened,' I cried, so happy to see him all in one piece, but furious at his making me worry so much.

'Nothing, my dear,' he laughed, 'nothing except that I just met your friend Pillete.'

And Luis told me this story:

It seems that he had got very thirsty on the drive down and had stopped at the plaza in Trujillo to get a beer. Naturally, he went into the Bar Imperio and Pillete at once realized he was a stranger. Not at all shy, he engaged Luis in conversation.

'Are you from Madrid?' he asked.

'Yes,' Luis replied.

'Ah, I know Madrid well,' said Pillete, anxious to dispel any notion that he was a mere country yokel. 'Yes, I have a number of very important friends in Madrid. Do you by any chance know a charming and very elegant lady—she's very important, I'm sure you must have heard of her—called la Condesa de Quintanilla?'

A little devil must have been whispering to Luis, for he decided to play it dumb.

'Mmm . . .,' he said non-committally.

'Well, she is a very good friend of mine and of my family. She is one of the most famous women in this area. We have come to know her because she is arranging and modernizing her *finca* near here—Pascualete, it is called. One of the finest in the region.'

'Really?' said Luis.

'*Si*, Señor, the Señora Condesa has taken the old *palacio* and— and she is bringing it back to life! Do you know—she has put in running water! Imagine! And bathrooms, and she is furnishing it with great elegance. And she has even installed an electric generator. Señor, you cannot imagine what it is to have electricity in that remote *finca*. Why there is not even a road to it.

'Of course, I know all this, Señor, because I am privileged to

51

The Discovery of Pascualete

be the friend of this great lady. I, Pillete, have helped her in every way as have my wife and five children and it has been a great pleasure to serve this extraordinary Condesa.'

'I am sure you must have helped greatly,' said Luis, hoping to urge him on.

'And what is more—the Condesa even shows movies every week to the people of the *finca*. I, Pillete, receive the film from Madrid for her and then I give the old film back to the man who brings it from Madrid. Imagine—they are showing these country people who have never seen a movie in their lives—they are showing them the Metro-Gol. The Metro-Gol!'*

Apparently the Metro-Gol was too much for Luis and he began laughing so hard that he had to confess to Pillete who he was, and after a few more drinks they were fast friends.

So Luis not only approved of my new friends, but he even had the effrontery a few weeks later to claim Pillete as his own discovery.

I must say I was relieved to be able to produce a real Spanish husband, at least to dilute a little the atmosphere of a crazy American woman I had surely created.

It was Luis who informed me that Pillete means 'rascal' in Spanish and that he had quite a devastating effect on the ladies. And even though Pillete was far from debonair and handsome, Candida was very jealous. Whenever Pillete was not around the bar, Candida sent little errand boys out looking for him. It used to amuse us tremendously to watch her walk out into the plaza, place her hands determinedly on her ample hips and give a piercing look in every direction to see if she could distinguish the squat figure of her husband. Little by little I realized there were reasons for her anxiety. It seems that Pillete had a girl-friend, a plump, dark gipsy, who lived in great style in a boarding-house in one of the old *palacios*, high on the hill above the plaza.

One evening when Luis returned particularly late to the *finca*, he told me that he had finally met the gipsy. Pillete had invited him to have a glass of beer with a friend. After walking up one of

* Pillete's way of saying Metro Goldwyn Mayer.

52

Pillete, the delightful Rascal of Trujillo

the serpentine streets towards the top of the city to a tumbledown palace, they knocked at a door with a round peephole which mysteriously opened before they were allowed to enter. Luis said that it was a very gay evening with Pillete's gipsy dancing *Flamenco* and Pillete's classic laugh booming loudly above the noisy guitar.

There was one dramatic moment when Pillete turned pale, for his son, who had been sent out by Candida to look for her straying husband, had finally tracked down Papa and was waiting in the patio below.

'Go back to the Plaza,' Pillete ordered his son, 'and tell your mother I am discussing a very serious business deal with the Señor Conde.'

That day Luis learned many interesting things about another side of life in Trujillo. We had noticed in the cinema a box on the balcony above, which was completely enclosed in curtains. When asked what it was for, we received an evasive answer, but Luis discovered that night that the box was reserved for Trujillo's prostitutes. These women in Trujillo had a much more restricted life than in the cities. They were segregated in one small section of the city, and there was an off-limits line which they were prohibited from crossing. If they had to do some shopping, they did so with their faces completely covered by thick veils and their only public amusement was the movies which they viewed from peepholes in the curtains of their box. In recent years prostitution has been outlawed in Spain and now, of course, the curtained box has disappeared.

The Club of Estremanian Farmers

NOW THAT PASCUALETE was beginning to take shape, I had more time to investigate another aspect of life in my strange new world. Although I was surrounded by animals and farming, my concept of that science remained somewhat vague. And my new friends at the Bar Imperio, being mostly farmers, spoke a special language of the trade which I could not understand.

Up to this point, I had not gone beyond the stage of admiring the attractive landscape and agreeable sounds around me. I liked looking at the flocks of sheep roaming the surrounding hills and listening to the music of their tinkling bells. At sundown, the children and I often stood at the balcony window upstairs watching the long lines of cattle stream into the patio below.

Often I rode my mare through fields of graceful wheat stalks which in the wake of the wind rolled like great green waves and rustled like the finest silk. In the distance, plantings of oats, barley and rye cut long swathes of chartreuse, turquoise and emerald green against the background of a deep blue sky. My eyes appreciated the beauty, but I could not tell the difference between one crop and another. Juan often laughed at me and even jolly Isidora would become smugly superior as she explained:

'No, no, Señora Condesita, those sprouts are not barley. They are oats.'

Obviously, I would never earn their esteem if I did not learn something about farming, but it was a dangerous subject to broach. No matter how carefully I phrased my questions I could tell from the way Juan and Primitivo shook their heads that they were appalled by my ignorance and most doubtful of ever enlightening me.

The Club of Estremanian Farmers

The difficulties and pitfalls of a farmer's life indeed were painted for me in the most sombre colours and I soon realized that it was nothing short of a miracle that any farmer manages to make ends meet. The picture was particularly gloomy in Estremadura. The summers were so dry that the sun burnt out all the natural pasturage.

'*Sí*, Señora Condesa, during the summer months we often have to march the animals two hundred miles north to find pasture,' Juan informed me.

In my first flush of agricultural enthusiasm, I bought just about every book available on the subject. All remained unread except the first three, over which I made great efforts and learned little. But I did read about an American grass which would grow tall and green in almost desert conditions. Juan was sceptical, but eventually he agreed to try it.

'I suppose there is no other way to teach the Señora Condesa farming than to let her make her own mistakes. But the Señora Condesa has my assurance that nothing—but nothing—will grow in Estremadura in the months of August and September without rain.'

We were standing on a small incline near the house. With his hat on his head and his feet firmly embedded in the earth, Juan had the self-confidence of a god and he continued to expound:

'Furthermore, our livestock is very special. These animals will not eat just anything. They are smart and they know what is good for them. In dry weather, any grass that might sprout from these seeds the Señora Condesa wishes to try would be weak and not to their taste at all. How could a grass that flourishes in August or September have the kind of nourishment and strength that God-fearing animals need?'

'But Juan, the wrapping of this seed package calls it "the ice cream of cattle". It says that American animals thrive on it and love it.'

'Well, I do not know what kind of animals there are in America, but one thing I am sure of—they are not like ours. For example,

The Discovery of Pascualete

these merino sheep of Estremadura are the best in the world and they are very, very particular about what they eat. Nevertheless, tomorrow the oxen will prepare the field and we will begin planting.'

(Of course, now I had to resign myself to months of waiting before any results would appear. And as was the case in all my early experiments in farming, my American pasture was a dismal burnt bare field. Nevertheless, I insisted on trying again and a year later it was so successful that a few sheep were able to stay home and feed off this American 'ice cream'.)

In general, however, Juan did a better job of converting me to his ways than I did of Americanizing him. Having the typical American faith in the printed word, I was an easy 'take' for the American farm magazines. There I read that one should specialize, so one morning I sprang my newly-discovered theory on Juan.

He shook his head patronizingly:

'That does not work in Estremadura. If it is a bad year for the sheep, it may be good for the cows and if it is bad for the pigs it will probably be good for the wheat. So we manage in that way never to have any years which are a complete loss financially.'

As all my suggestions came to naught, Primitivo one day took pity on me and came up with a brilliant idea.

'According to the Señor Conde's contract with Juan and his brothers, the livestock and the working of the fields belong to the tenants,' Primitivo explained. 'But there is a clause in that contract which permits the owners of the *finca* to possess some pigs and a family of sheep and goats. If the Señora Condesa really wants to learn something about animals, Juan could buy some for her at the next fair in Trujillo.'

When we discussed Primitivo's suggestion with Juan, he agreed it would be a good way to initiate me into the finer details of animal husbandry.

'The Señora Condesa can rest assured that I will buy for her the best animals in the fair,' said Juan.

'Oh, no,' I said firmly. 'That is not what I want at all. I want to go to the fair myself and buy the pigs.'

The Club of Estremanian Farmers

'But how will the Señora Condesa be able to tell one pig from another, if she will pardon the question?'

Finally, I persuaded Juan that if he would accompany me and give his valuable opinion, perhaps I might be able to learn.

A few weeks later we found ourselves at the famous cattle fair in Trujillo, one of the typical country fairs held throughout Spain. For centuries in Trujillo these fairs have taken place on the plains just outside the city walls.

Sprawled over the fair-grounds were cattle, pigs, sheep, horses, mules and donkeys herded together in different sections. Little covered wagons filled with gipsy families who specialize in selling horses added an exotic touch and under gaily striped awnings sat hordes of Estremanian farmers, drinking wine and eating bright red water melon. Aside from the gipsies, I was the only woman wandering around that great plain swarming with animals and shouting, gesticulating farmers. Every man at the fair carried a long gaudy cane which he used to point out the qualities or defects of each animal, so I immediately bought myself a stick, too.

My intention that day was to buy six pigs, as that was all I was allowed according to the contract, but I was constantly distracted on my way to the pig section by the panorama about me. Passing the area where the sheep were grouped in enclosures, I was amazed to count at least six drastically different colours of sheep. There were white sheep, grey sheep, orange sheep, pastel pink sheep, bright yellow sheep and muddy brown sheep. The most beautiful were the orange and pink ones, which reminded me of the paintings of the Spanish impressionist, Palencia. I had always thought the artist must be exaggerating the brilliant colours of the animals, but in Estremadura, at least, nature does not belie him. Of course, the omniscient Juan knew why.

'Each flock is the colour of the earth on which the sheep sleep,' Juan explained, 'and since the earth in Estremadura is so varied and has such strong colours, you can always tell where each sheep comes from. See the pink sheep over there? They are from Sierra de Fuentes where the earth is bright red, and here, these sheep nearest us are from La Cumbre where the terra cotta soil turns them orange.'

I asked which ones were from Pascualete, hoping that red or pink would be the answer.

'*Gracias a Dios*, in Pascualete the sheep are grey,' said Juan, 'because we have good soil. If you see orange or pink sheep, you know the earth they come from is poor.'

When we arrived at the pig section there was very little activity. The pigs were rooting noisily in assorted groups, each of which was guarded by a man who occasionally threw them bits of feed to keep them from mixing. There was every size from forty-pound porkers to little baby pigs.

Juan advised me we must walk nonchalantly among all the groups of pigs and not show any interest. When I saw some I liked, I was to listen to the price other people might be offering for them.

'Then you can talk a bit with the owner,' Juan said, 'discuss the difficulties of buying and selling these days—but do not show any particular desire for HIS pigs. He will tell you what price he has been offered, and he will say he has had many offers, but does not want to sell yet. Then move on to another group. Once we have passed through the whole section, we shall be in a good position to make an offer.'

Juan and I started ambling around, but just as he had predicted, I could not decide which pigs I wanted because they all looked identical to me. Now and then I found some especially nice plump ones and suggested to Juan that they were the best, but he always disagreed. Their udders or tails or noses or ears were not just right. Finally, we approached some pigs which, according to Juan, were the best he had seen.

We found the owner, and after the usual lengthy exchange of amenities, we managed to convey the proper degree of indifference. But my worry was the moment when I would have to inform the vendor that my purchase was to be only six pigs and not six hundred, which would have been more normal.

I could see Juan expected the bargaining to go very badly and

The Club of Estremanian Farmers

that I would end up paying for six pigs what he paid for sixteen, so I was determined not to lose face. The vendor was asking 300 pesetas ($7.10) per pig and gradually I beat him down. As we haggled over the last point, I permitted myself a moment of pride for the way I was carrying on this difficult final negotiation. However, I stopped, red-faced, when the young man said:

'Really, I have never seen a Condesa so upset about a half a peseta in my life!' and I discovered that I had been haggling over one cent each pig for the past fifteen minutes, much to the amusement of an enormous crowd which now surrounded me.

'Well, the Señora Condesa has struck a very good bargain,' said the vendor, 'and now how many pigs shall I separate for her?'

I mustered all my courage, strength and dignity, to answer as if it were the most normal thing in the world:

'I think I'll take six pigs today.'

The crowd roared as the poor vendor tried to hide his chagrin. And having spent the last quarter of an hour saving myself six cents, I walked off with my six little pigs which cost 260 pesetas each. I must have thought I was in Macy's, for I turned my back and walked on as if to say, 'Wrap them up and send them.'

Terribly self-satisfied, and trying to look as if I bought pigs every day, I walked along fancying I saw admiring looks wherever I went. Actually, these were only amused glances, for when I finally looked behind me, I saw my six little pigs following along single file! I blushed from confusion, but I did not dare ask Juan why those pigs followed so obediently at my heels. The next time I turned, however, my question was answered, as I saw Juan take a handful of grain from his pocket and drop little kernels in their path.

By the time spring came round again, my baby pigs had gained tremendously and I made a profit of 8,000 pesetas on their sale. When I calculated at this rate what I could do with six hundred pigs, I began to take agriculture seriously. I dreamed I walked into the Trujillo fair with six hundred fat pigs. I heard myself making brilliant remarks about their virtues, pointing expertly with my stick to their udders and snouts to verify my claims.

The Discovery of Pascualete

Then I walked out with my pockets full of pesetas, amidst the admiration of all the farmers of the area.

During that morning of my first country fair, two of my farmer friends Don Federico and Don Ignacio Hornedo invited me to have an aperitif at the Bar Imperio. Their first words to Pillete were:

'Imagine, Pillete, the Condesa de Quintanilla is the talk of the fair, for she bought her pigs at ten pesetas lower than anyone else.'

The bar was packed, but the beaming Pillete showed us to the only empty table. I was so delighted to be in the midst of all this activity and little did the Hornedo brothers realize to what extent I was impressed by it all and how grateful I was for their introduction into this new world. Infected by the hubbub and excitement around me, I found myself recounting my purchase of the morning, just like everyone else. Now I was a true farmer of Estremadura!

PART TWO

THE HISTORY OF
PASCUALETE

6

Alvaro, my first Historical Love

I N MY NICE COSY BED in front of the crackling fire, while
I lay still and snug listening to the ghostly night noises, I
used to wonder what kind of people must have lived in
Pascualete. Who were they? I wondered particularly about the
man who had planned those beautiful Romanesque arches downstairs, the man to whom had belonged the very mysterious coat
of arms of the five roses which I had seen that first night in the
floor—that *escudo* that I encountered in every place I went,
especially the enormous one carved in aged greenish stone over
the entrance arch.

Many times I had asked Luis to tell me what he knew about
Pascualete—if his family had bought it and where the *escudo* of
the five roses could have come from. He told me he suspected the
finca had been in his family for a long time, but the *escudo* remained a mystery to us, for apparently it was not a family coat of
arms.

I knew that in Spain each noble family name bears a coat of
arms, but in cases where there are no sons to carry on the family
name certain coats of arms become extinct. Therefore I was not
completely discouraged about the possibility of the *escudo* of
five roses having belonged in some distant period to my husband's
family. The property and even titles could have been passed on
by daughters, while the *escudo* was superseded by those of their
husbands.

Early one morning, with the idea of finding someone who
could put me on the track of Pascualete's ancient owners, I
directed my jeep (Luis finally had been obliged to buy me a
vehicle which could withstand the jolts of our cowpath) towards
Trujillo and the Bar Imperio. My indispensable Pillete informed

63

The History of Pascualete

me that the person in Trujillo who knew most about history was the old priest, Juan Tena, head of the municipal archives. He assured me that no one had read as many books as Padre Tena and that he had even written some kind of book about people dead hundreds of years ago. There was no doubt in Pillete's mind that Padre Tena was the only person in the universe who could help me.

Anxious to make the acquaintance of this fabulous sage, I urged Pillete to take me to him.

'Oh no, Padre Tena does not like to be interrupted in the midst of his reading. He might be in one of the convents where he has certain daily religious obligations; or he might even be in the house of the Widow Ramirez, who has been dying for a week now and who finds great solace in the Padre's prayers. Or he might be in the old Roman castle up on the hill, copying some strange markings in the old stones of the building.'

He was indeed a busy and important person, and very difficult to find.

'Just sit at this little table in the bar near the window and have a *café con leche* and sooner or later the Señora Condesa will see him crossing the plaza, and I will then present her to him.'

I had no choice but to resign myself to what seemed to me Pillete's very inefficient method of getting things done. The *café con leche* appeared. My faithful old bootblack, the moment he spotted me sitting down, came running over carrying his wooden stool in one hand and his box of shoe polishes in the other, with his usual introduction:

'I cannot permit the Señora Condesa to walk about Trujillo with those dirty shoes, and even if it must be at my own expense, I will take upon myself this obligation.'

I looked down to see what dust could possibly have collected upon my old country Oxfords which Maria had polished to shining brilliance five minutes before I left for Trujillo. As usual, neither the ride nor the twenty or so steps I had taken from the car through the plaza had greatly impaired Maria's work, but it was

Padre Tena in a corner of the Plaza of Trujillo standing near the
statue of Francisco Pizarro

Don Alfonso in front of the church of Santa Marta

Alvaro, my first Historical Love

such fun to listen to my old friend's conversation that I put up a shiny foot and he went to work.

He first made a thorough mess of Maria's efforts by slapping on all kinds of grease and then busily polished the daylights out of the old leather. I shuddered to think what a disapproving glare I would receive from my pinchpenny *guardesa* if she could see me wasting three pesetas in this fashion, but I appeased my conscience with the thought that so much attention would undoubtedly make these shoes last a lifetime.

Just as I was wondering how many *cafés con leche* it would take to see Father Tena appear in the plaza, Pillete came running over and pointed to a lone figure in long black skirts crossing the plaza. I nearly knocked over the bootblack in my haste and we both ran out into the bright sunny town square.

Padre Tena's small sparkling blue eyes regarded me quizzically as Pillete explained that I had an urgent matter to discuss with him. Although tall and well-built, his back was as bent as any of the Estremanian farmers, and his wrinkled pale face was kind and pleasant. With few words he indicated that I should follow him and we continued through the narrow streets to the great old palace which held the city archives.

'Well, Condesa,' said the companion at my side, 'So you are interested in finding out something about the history of Pascualete. I know your old palace well, because I stop there each year on my way to Santa Marta when I go to say mass on the day of their patron saint. You certainly have many interesting things to uncover in that old house. I have always felt that its origin is thirteenth century and its history undoubtedly must be very much linked with that of this noble city of Trujillo.'

His voice was soft and warm and I was charmed by his picturesque appearance. His long, white hair hung untidily under the round, straight-brimmed priest's hat and his ample black skirts showed signs of many years wear. But he glanced at me now and then out of the corner of his eye as he walked along with an amused glint that disturbed me. I could not tell whether he was pleased or making fun of my inquisitiveness.

The History of Pascualete

'Unfortunately Trujillo's noble families have long since left this city, but their mark is still here. Do you know, Condesa, that some of the greatest names in the history of our country came from here. The Chaves, the Carvajals, the Sotomayers—great Spanish names those. And this was once a very rich city also. There are few towns in Spain that can boast so many palaces as Trujillo. What do you have in Madrid? Nothing but modern buildings. There is no real history in a city that was founded only four hundred years ago.'

We mounted two flights of wide stone steps and then a narrow winding wooden staircase which creaked ominously. My new friend pulled out of his pocket a conglomeration of old keys of enormous weight and size and proceeded to open several doors, all of which led into rooms crowded with shelves bent under the weight of many yellowed manuscripts. I followed his shuffling footsteps as he placed two chairs at a table near the window and offered me a seat. This window looked out upon ancient red-tiled rooftops and down into an old patio where scraggly chickens were pecking about the ruins of some beautiful columns.

An expression of tenderness came over Father Tena's pale parchment-like face, as he made a gesture with his hand towards the view.

'I love very dearly this ancient city and its people, perhaps because I feel I know it better than anyone. For forty-five years in this same room I have studied these limitless manuscripts. I have spent many more hours deep in these old papers than would be necessary for a simple archivist such as I am, because I have made such close friends that I never tire of learning more about them. I not only know Trujillans and their parents and grand-parents but in many cases I know these families for twenty generations.'

The utter silence of the attic room, musty with the odour of old manuscripts, was broken only by Father Tena's voice as he told me many stories of Trujillo, and before I realized it, two fascinating hours had slipped by.

Several days later, as I climbed the narrow steps to my now

regular appointment with Father Tena, I could see him standing in the doorway with a little more sparkle than usual in his pale blue eyes.

'I have just found references to the sale of your property in an old volume and I thought you might be interested in reading it. This transaction took place in the year 1558.'

I rushed to look at the book in his hand, but Padre Tena said gently, 'Not so much haste, daughter, first I think you should understand the background of the period.

'In 1556 the great Spanish King Carlos V, exhausted from his many wars throughout Europe and against the Turks, renounced his throne in favour of his son Philip II with the desire to retire from the world and devote his last years to meditation. He remembered that in his dominions there was a Spain and in that Spain there was an Estremadura and he shut up his glory in the Monastery of Yuste, which is not very far from here. Perhaps he discovered, as you have, my child, that this sky is more heaven than any other and in its nights one can feel closer to our Creator.'

Father Tena was accustomed to giving lengthy sermons without interruption, and I was beginning to despair of his ever getting to the subject—but finally he picked up the old volume and I listened fascinated as his gentle voice went on to read the following tale.

'The constant wars of this great Emperor had so depleted the Crown revenues that in 1558 his son King Philip II, who was himself involved in costly wars in Flanders, was obliged to raise money by selling certain Crown properties. Philip therefore issued instructions to offer for sale six huge tracts of land near Trujillo, among which was the estate of Santa Marta de Magasca, some 150,000 acres. This . . .'

'But, Padre, that must be the village of Santa Marta—why that is Pascualete!'

'Just a minute, my child. Let me finish. My, my, such haste,' he reprimanded, and continued reading.

'This being the era of serfdom, the inhabitants were sold at a price of 16,000 maravedis* each, along with the land, which fetched 4,000 ducados† each league, the peasants thereby becoming vassals of the Lord of the property.'

'But, Padre, doesn't it say who bought the property?' I interrupted again.

'Yes, child, it comes in the next paragraph. Santa Marta de Magasca was bought by a certain Alvaro de Loaisa, who was then given the title of Señor (Lord) of Santa Marta.'

The book went on to say that the district of Santa Marta had in the centremost point one piece of about three thousand acres called Pascualete, on which was an old palace and certain farm enclosures for cattle. The only village in this area was also named Santa Marta. It was composed of fifty heads of families and was located near the farm buildings of the *finca* Pascualete.

'The buyers of the six areas took possession of their lands and in the most central point placed their family *escudos* and built their walled-in manor houses,' Padre Tena concluded.

As I bounced over the rutty cowpath on my way back to the ranch, I mused over the morning's revelations. A million new questions came to my mind. How could I wait until tomorrow morning to get back to my friend the old priest?

Who was Alvaro de Loaisa?

Late that night, once again in my bed, I wanted so much to pry through the black separation of these past four centuries to reach this Alvaro Loaisa, that the eerie whining of the wind and other ghostly night noises made me feel he must be very near.

I could see Alvaro, tall and distinguished, his hair black and abundant, as was his beard which grew high on his cheekbones and tended to elongate the narrow face. He wore the typical costume of a Spanish gentleman of the sixteenth century—a metal breastplate, short balloon pants, his legs in stockings, and around his neck was a high collar or ruff.

* A maravedi was a coin made of copper and gold issued in Burgos during the reign of Alfonso the Wise, the value of which was approximately one quarter of one peseta, or 25 centimos.

† Ducado was a gold coin used towards the end of the 16th century and was worth from 5 to 7 pesetas.

Alvaro, my first Historical Love

Indeed he seemed so real that I had a long conversation with him. I hated Maria the next morning when she scoffed at my suggestions of ghosts in Pascualete, although she was quick to make the classic Latin sign of devil's horns and touch wood.

'The slow footsteps the Señora Condesa hears at night are no more than the flutterings of small birds who find their way through holes in the thick stone wall to make their nests in the small attic under the roof. And although at Pascualete we have few mice, who can say that one does not present himself now and then and decide to scamper back and forth through the attic. The strong wind too, often makes the loose shutters groan.'

'But Maria, how can a mouse or a bird make noises as loud as the ones I hear at night? They sound like a heavy man's footsteps.'

Maria then gave me a quizzical look and remarked cautiously:

'Well, that is true. I have heard these very same sounds at night and when I first came to live at Pascualete they used to frighten me. But Señora Condesa, they must be very good ghosts because I have never met any of them and they certainly keep to themselves.'

On my way to Trujillo the next morning I reviewed my questions for Father Tena. I did not even stop to say 'Good morning' to Candida and Pillete as I hurriedly parked in the plaza. Fortunately it was much too early for my bootblack to be out of bed, so I also avoided that delay.

As I walked through the big door to the archives, the old gateman greeted me.

'The Señora Condesa is even earlier than the good Padre,' so I had to wait.

When Father Tena finally appeared, he began as usual to discuss the beautiful morning and asked me as we mounted the stairs together how the sheep were managing with this drought, etc. Oh, what a slow, calm man!

When I finally got the chance, I attacked.

'Padre, to what family does the *escudo* of five roses belong?'

By now he was sitting in his worn old wooden armchair, and

he very slowly leaned back and closed the book in front of him.

'Daughter, that is the *escudo* of the noble family of Loaisa, who came to Trujillo in the fifteenth century, having originally come from France. You will notice that around the five roses is a border.'

'Yes, I couldn't quite make out what the border was,' I answered. 'It looks like fleurs-de-lis cut in half.'

'You are exactly right, my child. You see, a member of the Loaisa family died while defending the life of the King of France from three men who attacked him. As a reward, the King made him a gift of three gold pieces in the form of fleurs-de-lis—the royal insignia of the Kings of France. At the same time, the King ordered that these fleurs-de-lis be added to the coat of arms of the descendants of this noble man. And so that is why ever after the five roses were bordered with three half fleurs-de-lis on each side.'

As soon as I returned to the farm I pulled out the red leather *Guide to Nobility* and looked up Luis' family title of Marqués de Santa Marta. There I found that this title was a continuation of the Señorio de Santa Marta which had been granted in 1558 to Alvaro de Loaisa and which was raised to a Marquisate in 1737. So Alvaro de Loaisa was our direct ancestor!

I ran all over the house looking for Luis. I burst in upon him just as he was in the midst of arranging some new paintings on a wall downstairs.

'Luis, what do you think! Alvaro Loaisa is your great-great-great . . . grandfather and Pascualete must have been inherited by your family all those four hundred years from the time he owned it!'

Luis opened his mouth to speak. I was waiting for my moment of praise.

'Primitivo, that upper left-hand picture is a little too far to the left. You had better take it down and measure the distance,' he said.

'But Luis, have you heard what I just told you?'

Alvaro, my first Historical Love

'Now Aline, how could I or anyone else possibly care who was my grandfather four hundred years ago? We had to come from some place, I dare say you had a grandfather of your own four hundred years ago.'

I went slowly back upstairs, not too depressed by Luis' lack of enthusiasm. I was already wondering how I could find out more about those Loaisas who had lived at Pascualete four centuries ago.

7

Exploring the Roman ruins at Pascualete
with a French Abbé

UNFORTUNATELY, I could not rush back in to Trujillo
to fire more questions at Padre Tena, for the week-end
had come and we were about to receive one of our first
guests at Pascualete.

Our visitor was Madrid's most distinguished foreign ecclesi-
astic, the delight of Spanish society, and a friend of ours for many
years. A brilliant, learned man and a stimulating conversationalist,
Monseigneur was also an avid sportsman, and we had invited him
to Pascualete to shoot.

As his big black limousine rolled into our dusty patio, Primitivo
ran out to stand at attention, trying desperately to look dignified
in the midst of children, barking dogs and scattering chickens.
An immaculately dressed chauffeur in shiny black boots and
fancy gold-embroidered hat sprang out and with a great flourish
opened the door, revealing a beaming round red face looking
out towards us. Radiating his usual charm, Monseigneur
emerged majestically and came towards me with outstretched
hands.

'My dear Aline, what a treat to be able to visit you here in your
beautiful country place.'

He made a grand gesture at my bedraggled patio as if he were
viewing the gardens of Versailles. He held his tri-cornered shiny
black hat under his left arm and his immaculate black cassock
swished in the wind while the long crimson bands of his wide
cummerbund made moving flashes of colour about him. Even the
patio animals—to say nothing of the children—stood back in
awe.

Exploring the Roman ruins at Pascualete with a French Abbé

As Luis and I led our old friend into the house he glanced up at the stone escudo above the door.

'This house has a marvellous atmosphere,' he said. 'One can just feel the strong unbending character of the Spaniards typified by that *escudo* which must have been here for hundreds of years.'

Later, as we were sitting down to take a glass of sherry in front of the fireplace, he looked down and exclaimed:

'But what is this I am stepping on? Do bring the light closer.'

Heedless of his flowing skirts he dropped to his knees on the bare stone floor and began to rub carefully with his fingers the grooves in a long flat stone to remove the dust.

'How remarkable! Why, this is an ancient Roman tombstone and very legible at that!'

His quick natural enthusiasm gave way to his love of drama and in a deep commanding voice he began to translate slowly the worn inscription of the stone slab:

CAENUS, SON OF CAVCIRIUS, HERE LIES BURIED.
MAY THE EARTH REST LIGHTLY ON YOU. HIS
DAUGHTER VALERIA SET UP THIS MONUMENT.

Monseigneur stood up and declared, 'This really is an old house you have here. That tombstone is almost two thousand years old.'

As I listened to his words once again I was overwhelmed by the mystery of this house. More and more, it seemed, the ghosts of yesterday were trying to lure me back into an ancient world. I remembered the first day we had seen those Latin inscriptions in various parts of the house.

'Monseigneur, I have seen several of these stones in the house and even in the cattle barns. Although my college Latin is pretty much forgotten, they looked very Roman to me, but I have never dared let my imagination believe that they might have been here since the time of the Roman colonization in Spain.'

'My dear Aline, wherever you find Roman tombstones in Spain you can be certain that there was Roman life in that very spot. But this is fascinating—will you show me some of these other stones?'

The History of Pascualete

Leaving our sherry forgotten on the table in front of the fire, we ran like children up the stone steps to my room. Even Luis, who usually reserved his enthusiasm for his flower garden or some old bustard which he had just shot, ran up behind us. It was difficult to place a light so that the Abbé could read the lettering in the dark tunnel of the window opening and he was obliged to lie on his back on a table with his head resting on the stone ledge in order to read the inscription:

PUBLIUS RUTILIUS MUNUS, 55 YEARS OLD, HERE
LIES BURIED. MAY THE EARTH REST LIGHTLY ON
YOU. HIS SON HAD THIS MONUMENT SET UP.

After dinner that same night we went through the dark cattle sheds, looking for more Roman stones. As Isidora's husband, Paco, lit our way with an oil lamp, Monseigneur began to tell the story of the Roman conquest of Spain.

'After almost two hundred turbulent years of warfare, the Romans settled down to an intensive agricultural exploitation of this hitherto savage country. They cleared entire forests to prepare the land for cultivation, wells were dug and seeds and equipment were brought from Italy. By the second century A.D.,' Monseigneur continued, 'this colony of Rome was at the peak of her civilization. Why—she even provided Rome with great emperors such as Trajan, philosophers such as Seneca and many writers and poets. Estremadura was one of the most important agricultural areas, since it provided great wealth in wool and wheat.'

Briefly, he explained that the Roman government, in order to encourage immigration and agriculture, had offered tracts of land and equipment to those Romans who would be willing to cultivate it. These Roman ranches or farms, called *latifundios*, were built much like those in existence today in Estremadura. The main house was built around a rectangular patio and consisted of a strong stone building with small windows and high ceilings.

In the tunnel-like vaulted cowshed Paco, who had until then been standing like a statue, suddenly came to life. As he began to

Exploring the Roman ruins at Pascualete with a French Abbé

speak, the light in his trembling hand made jagged flashes and shadows and I realized that Paco was shy and excited to find himself addressing such an important personage.

'Pardon me, Your Excellency, but does Your Excellency think Pascualete might once upon a time have been a farm of these Roman people?'

'Yes, my son, it might have been, at that. There are certainly many indications. These feed troughs, for example, of hard granite are the identical shape that the Romans used and one can easily see by the deep grooves on the side where the cattle feed that they are worn by many centuries' use.'

'Well, I declare! My wife Isidora is quite smart. She has always remarked about these strange writings. She knows how to read and says that these letters do not look anything at all like the language we Spaniards use today, that there must have been some very strange people living here a long, long time ago.'

I now directed my guest into an adjoining large vaulted room on the ground floor, which was stacked high with bales of sheep's wool, sacks of seed and odd pieces of farm equipment.

'Look,' said the Abbé enthusiastically, stretching his arm along the huge mantel of the fireplace, 'One can see that these arched doorways and this fireplace with its immense granite blocks might have been here from the very time that Pascualete was a Roman *latifundio*! Besides, this property was very well situated for a Roman agricultural development. It is only twenty kilometres from the Roman town of Turgalium, which today is Trujillo, and only thirty-two kilometres from the great Roman centre of Castra Caecilia, now Caceres.

'After the Romans lost their control over Spain in A.D. 450 and barbarian tribes came in from the north and began to fight each other, these Roman constructions may have fallen into disrepair. Perhaps later on others once again took to farming here and profited from certain walls and floors for their new farm buildings,' he added.

The next morning, Monseigneur insisted on exploring more before shooting. The back of the house was still in its original disorder, for I had not yet had time to plan what I wanted to do with it. But Monseigneur decided for me.

'Aline, do you realize that some of those broken columns are Roman. I'm sure the missing pieces must be lying around the property. Think what a lovely terrace you could have by using those columns as supports!'

Later in the morning Monseigneur managed to shoot the biggest bustard we had yet seen—just a few paces from the house. And before leaving, when he again remarked about the beauty of our house, I knew he meant it.

8

The Origins of the name 'Pascualete'

WITH EACH NEW VISITOR, I discussed and studied the architecture of Pascualete and gradually it became obvious that certain parts of the house were of a period much previous to the sixteenth century and my new friend Alvaro de Loaisa. The entrance arch was definitely thirteenth century, as well as Romanesque doors and window frames. Now I began to harass Padre Tena for thirteenth and fifteenth century manuscripts from the endless town files. It became painfully obvious to me that Father Tena had many things to do other than sit in the municipal archives with me and read old manuscripts.

I followed him throughout the city, even on his rounds to the different convents, and generally made myself such a nuisance that I suppose in desperation he resorted to lending me old books of his own which I could read and would keep me busy at the *finca* searching out information about our property and ancestors.

It was in one of these books that I discovered the reason for our *finca's* peculiar name. Actually, I had not realized it was a strange name until I began mentioning Pascualete to our friends who invariably remarked, 'What a pity your nice *finca* should have such an ugly name.'

To my American ears the fall of Spanish sounds has always seemed extremely attractive and it rather startled me that Pascualete should be less euphonious to Spaniards. But it seems that Pascualete has a rather undignified meaning in Spanish as it is the nickname for the proper name of Pascual. So to a Spaniard Pascualete sounds just as incongruous as for us to call a large centuries old estate in America, 'Buster', or 'Jackie'.

The History of Pascualete

Padre Tena's book recounted the following story:

It seems that in 1280 a certain Pascual Ruiz owned a large farm about ten kilometres, as the crow flies, from Trujillo.

Pascual Ruiz was extremely tall and broad-shouldered with a ruddy complexion and a shock of strong blond hair. He was not married, but he loved to have his house full of friends and there were always extra places at his table for as many people as might arrive. He was a man of a very happy nature, always ready with a funny story, but also capable of the most violent fury if the occasion demanded.

The apple of Pascual's eye was an orphaned nephew whom he had raised almost from birth. When the lad was eighteen he was sent off to the University of Salamanca to study. In Salamanca he got himself into a gambling scrape and, frightened of his doting uncle's quick temper, he dared not ask him for the money to pay off his debts.

So this nephew decided to sell the *finca* he owned bordering that of his uncle Pascual, to a prominent Trujillan family called Orellana. The boy thought that by the time his uncle discovered the matter many months would have passed and he would be far removed from Pascual's wrath.

But Pascual heard of the sale immediately and was furious. He told his nephew that, first, as he was still not of age, he had no legal right to sell any property without permission of his guardian; secondly, had the nephew offered the property to his uncle first, he most certainly would have given him a better price than anyone else.

And Pascual also made it known that since this piece of property was almost entirely surrounded by his own, he had no intention of allowing the Orellanas to take possession. He told the boy that he would pay the same price as the Orellanas, but that he never wished to see him again.

The Orellanas, fully aware that Pascual Ruiz would not tolerate the breaking up of this large tract of family property, equipped themselves with many horses and men in order to take over by force if necessary. On approaching their property they

The Origins of the name 'Pascualete'

found Pascual Ruiz surrounded by hundreds of his labourers and friends.

'I do not want to spill blood,' Pascual shouted, 'but I have no intention of letting anyone else take possession of this property. Surely the noble family of Orellana will understand that this has been the ill-considered action of an immature child. I urge you to request the return of your money and forget the whole matter.'

The Orellanas retreated that day without bloodshed, but they never gave up trying to claim their rich property.

A year later Pascual married a beautiful young girl from Trujillo. He was fifty-five at the time, and of course, wanted an heir, so the birth of a son shortly afterwards was an occasion of great rejoicing.

The boy was nicknamed Pascualete (little Pascual) and lived at the *finca* with his mother and father until he reached the age of ten, when he was sent to La Gramatica, the only school in Trujillo.

On certain week-ends and holidays Pascual Ruiz used to pick up his son from school. On one of these occasions Diego de Orellana, known as a thoroughly bad character and a hothead, hid himself in a doorway on a street near the school. It is not clear whom he meant to kill, but at any rate, as father and son passed by, Diego de Orellana killed the ten-year-old Pascualete.

Five years later, when the head of the house of Orellana and his eldest son, 'a good and loyal man', as the book described him, were returning from a near-by town, the father heard the noise of horsemen and, turning to look behind, excitedly cried to his son that he believed Pascual and his followers were about to overtake them. Orellana's son insisted that his father take his own fast horse which could easily outdistance Pascual. He convinced his father that all Pascual's grievances against the Orellana family were directed against the head of the house alone and if his father would take the horse and go to Trujillo there would be no danger. This was done and in no time the father was at a safe distance, but the younger Orellana was easily overtaken by Pascual and his men. A battle by sword followed and Pascual, although well on in his sixties, killed the son of Orellana.

Hardly a decade went by in Trujillo without one or two assassinations after that and thereby began a feud which lasted two centuries, and which eventually involved all the important families of Trujillo as they were forced to take sides.

There was no doubt in my mind that this feud had originated on our *finca*. The property bordering ours is called Pascual Ruiz and our own carries the unusual nickname of the small boy who was murdered and we are just about ten kilometres as the crow flies from Trujillo.

9

Palaeography and a New World

NOW I KNEW that Pascualete had Roman origins and as far back as the thirteenth century was the home of a Spanish nobleman named Pascual Ruiz. But there was a big gap between him and Alvaro de Loaisa and I knew nothing about the man I still considered my first historical love.

Father Tena shook his head discouragingly when I asked him to help me trace the two families.

'My child, you cannot expect that Trujillo's past city clerks would have kept card indexes of all past inhabitants,' he said for the hundredth time. 'The purpose of municipal archives was to record births and deaths, and to file legal disputes and ownerships of property.'

'Then,' I begged, 'find me the legal documentation for Pascualete. That would certainly tell us who owned the property up to the time of Alvaro de Loaisa.'

Father Tena, by now completely fed up with my questions, pulled out a stack of dusty manuscripts.

'Very well, if you have patience, the only place you might discover something would be in one of these, but you will have to do it by yourself.'

As I began to struggle over the almost illegible markings on the ancient papers, I noticed the priest was standing quietly in a darkened corner of the attic room, observing me. It was not until I got up indignant after spending five minutes fighting with the centuries-old script that I noticed he was shaking with silent laughter.

'Father, how am I going to make any sense out of these? I cannot read one letter!'

He laughed out loud and said:

The History of Pascualete

'I wondered what you would do when you got face to face with palaeography. Of course you cannot read it, it is old Spanish and only the few people who have studied this science are able to translate those documents.'

He seemed thoroughly amused by my misery and I began to think that maybe he was not so nice after all, when he sat down and took a piece of paper from the table and began to scribble something that looked like an address. He glanced up at me now with his usual fatherly smile.

'Really, child, you are getting into deep water when you aspire to decipher documents unread for the past four centuries or more. I am the only one in Trujillo who understands this science and I would gladly help you, but I have not the time. I fear neither your American energy nor your American belief that all secrets can be unravelled are sufficient to provide you with the patience you would need to learn.'

'How long will it take?'

He handed me his little piece of paper.

'I suppose it is useless for me to waste my time discouraging you. Here you have the address of the *archivista* of Caceres. He is a busy man and may have no time to give you lessons, but you can go to see him for yourself and tell him you are my friend.'

I did not see Father Tena for a long time after that. I did not even feel guilty at having abandoned my friend. I had no time.

There were no more shopping tours to Trujillo—no more chats with Pillete and Candida. I spent every day in Caceres bent over endless pages of crazy letters with a magnifying glass in my hand and an aching back. My teacher barely received a 'Good morning' from me in my haste to get to work. At night I studied until my eyes closed with exhaustion. Now and then I was obliged to go to Madrid, for there were parties and children's problems and a home to keep running, but I begrudged the moments spent away from the crumbling yellow pages and the faded hieroglyphics.

Luis was convinced that he had married the only useless American woman in existence.

Palaeography and a New World

'I did not complain when you were taking flamenco lessons every day, or when you decided you could run my office better than anyone else. You never have had time to remember to order flowers for the house—you are useless in the kitchen and never have five minutes to spare with the cook. The servants have broken so many glasses and dishes that we have practically nothing to eat off, but you have no time to go to the store to order more. What do you do? Spend weeks buried in Caceres, of all places, learning palaeography which will serve for nothing! Why can't you study in Madrid if you must take lessons in something? And you look awful—pale and tired.' I pictured myself growing crinkly half-shut eyes like Padre Tena from hours of straining over minute medieval letters.

'You American women spend your life studying and you know nothing. Here in Spain girls do not go to college, but they speak three languages perfectly and they stay in their homes all day long and like it.'

And so he complained, but I knew that secretly he was amused. Every now and then I would overhear him telling someone, 'You know, Aline is studying palaeography.'

Socially it had a great effect. My admirers changed greatly in age and appearance, they were now all over sixty, wore eyeglasses and knew something about palaeography. I could not bear a party unless I could find someone who could tell me something new about Estremanian history.

When I next arrived at the plaza in Trujillo I was greeted by a very hurt Pillete and Candida.

'So, the Señora Condesa prefers Caceres to our city. Not once has she come here in all her trips to the *finca*. Is it possible we have not attended her well? What have we done? What is wrong?'

'Nothing is wrong, I love Trujillo better than any place in the world, but I had to take lessons in Caceres. I have been working.'

I had been dying for the moment I could show off in front of Padre Tena. He heard me pounding up his squeaky stairs and was standing up to greet me when I entered.

'Well, well, it is about time——,' he began.

The History of Pascualete

'Father, I have no time for courtesies—pick out any manuscript you like, the more difficult the better.'

He pointed to a pile opened on his table, 'Try one of these.'

I sat down and recited as fast as I could in a loud and important voice the usual introduction:

'Know ye all who this letter may read that Juan Perez, inhabitant of this very loyal and noble city of Trujillo . . .'

I continued on to the bottom of the page before I looked up into his nice blue eyes.

I went back to the *finca* that night hugging a dirty old pile of manuscripts Father Tena had prepared for me and I did not go to sleep until very late. Nor did I for many nights after that. My documents went to Madrid with me, to the hairdresser with me, on any trip with me. It was a world I could not bear to be separated from for long.

It was a world stimulated by the fabulous discoveries of a new continent and harassed at home by the tentacles of the Inquisition. My papers concerned only Loaisas in the sixteenth century, but each one's life revealed a gripping story (see Appendix B).

Indeed before I finished, I knew many Loaisas intimately and they were an impressive family, but nowhere could I find anything about Alvaro. Why was he so elusive?

In desperation I hit on another method of attack. It used to be the custom to bury illustrious citizens in a place of honour in the floors of churches and since I had seen several tombstones with the *escudo* of five roses in the floor of the church of Santa Maria in Trujillo, I thought I might find the burial place of Alvaro de Loaisa there.

I began to spend a lot of time creeping round the church floor with a pail of water and an old scrubbing brush. The caretaker, a bent and decrepit old fellow, was most helpful in splashing water over the stones I indicated, while I brushed them carefully and copied their inscriptions into a notebook. In many cases the *escudos* and dates were so worn I could not distinguish them and although now and again I found a friend, I did not find Alvaro.

Seeing that I was becoming very unhappy about my quest for

Palaeography and a New World

Alvaro's dates, Father Tena suggested that I visit the little church of San Francisco where the sacristan might allow me to see the old registers.

'We know, my child, that the Loaisas must have been baptized in the cathedral of Santa Maria, high on the summit of the hill. However, in 1809, Napoleon's troops sacked and so destroyed the church that its ancient registers were sent to the church ·of San Francisco, where they have been lodged ever since,' he explained.

With Father Tena's note in hand I walked through the winding streets and up the hill to the impressive doors of the church of San Francisco. I paused just inside to breathe in the agreeable scent of incense and noted that as usual a few women had stopped during their morning marketing and were kneeling with black veil-covered heads near the front altar. Only slight gleams of light managed to filter through the old stained-glass windows, so that coming from the bright sunlight of the street, it took me several moments to find the door to the sacristy at the opposite end of the church. There I saw a wrinkled priest in a dusty black habit who rose and removed his glasses as he asked what he could do for me.

I showed him Father Tena's note and was directed to several open shelves where many dusty manuscripts were piled helter-skelter. He confessed that he had not had time to arrange these papers and from the amount of dust collected upon them it looked as though no one else had either, since 1809 when they had arrived there. The clouds of dust made us cough profusely as each book was disturbed and finally a little altar boy was sent out to look for a dustcloth so that we could make out the dates marked on the covers.

I began with one manuscript which started in 1502 and the old priest picked up another which began in 1514. Neither of us having any success, we finally pulled out another stack of papers dated 1483 which showed that these books were not kept in any special form.

Almost on the last page I saw the entry I was looking for.

The History of Pascualete

There it stated that in the year 1494, on the sixth of September to Pedro de Loaisa and Luisa de Tapia was born a son, Alvaro.

I suddenly could no longer feel my tired back and I wanted desperately to continue until I found the entry of his death. By this time there was a long queue of people who had come to call on the sacristan lined up in his doorway and I realized that I was holding up the normal events of the day. I assured him that I could continue my search alone and started with a book which began in 1557, knowing that Alvaro had to be very much alive when he bought Pascualete the following year. Very shortly afterwards, in 1563, I came across the entry marking the death of Don Alvaro de Loaisa, Señor de Santa Marta. I walked out of that quiet church feeling as if I had just lost a great friend.

The old priest noticed my tragic face, for he asked what was the matter.

'He died,' I answered in a trance.

Apparently Alvaro had bought Pascualete at the end of his life when he was sixty-four years old. How strange that seemed to me! I had always visualized him as a young man placing his *escudo* over the entrance arch and overseeing the construction of the lovely vaulted ceilings of the first floor. Still Alvaro remained a mystery. Perhaps he too had travelled to the New World. I had to know more.

10

Adventures in Santa Marta

URING THOSE EARLY DAYS at Pascualete I developed a special affection for the little village of Santa Marta, whose history was so intimately connected with that of the *finca*.

I supposed that the present population were descendants of the people who settled there two thousand years ago under the Romans. I also knew that when Alvaro de Loaisa bought the property in 1558 there were fifty families living there. Clearly, the serfs of Alvaro de Loaisa were also the ancestors of the two hundred and fifty families now inhabiting Santa Marta. Looking at them, I could never quite determine whether their origin was Arab, Celtic, or Roman. Most probably they were a mixture of all these bloods for they were of medium height, dark skinned, mostly with green eyes and light brown hair.

The Santa Martans are an industrious, peace-loving people, and I became very fond of them, even their difficult old priest. Much too often I would see a familiar little grey *burro* kicking up puffs of yellow dust along the winding path from Santa Marta. On his patient back rode the crotchety ageing village priest, Padre Remigio, with an open umbrella to shield him from the strong sun in one hand and the folds of his long black frock clutched in the other.

He was a bundle of grief and sad stories. He was always in need of money and always had some particularly sad tale to tell about one of his sinning parishioners. Even in Madrid I could not escape the badgering of Padre Remigio because long pages of lavish poetry would follow me by mail, written in the old priest's meticulous and elaborate script. It was a strange and very free verse and it invariably carried the same message. He needed money.

The History of Pascualete

This bad-tempered, bent old man was the terror of the village and during his reign the devotion of the people was indeed very slight.

One Sunday we took Luis' uncle, the Marqués del Merito, to Santa Marta to attend Mass. Visitors were invariably amused by the quaint village church. It has a low, tunnel-like entrance leading into a high round nave. Evidently the church had once been octagonal, was subsequently partly destroyed and in rebuilding, the townsfolk had simply closed in what remained of the majestic original building and had added the curious lower front part.

Just as we arrived several small boys who were scrambling about on the roof began to pull wildly on the ancient chain of the church bell and a hoarse clanging resounded throughout the stone village. Peps Merito, who had been watching attentively, turned to me and remarked:

'You know, it is a pity such an ancient bell should be cracked. Why don't you and Luis take it to Madrid and have it repaired?'

Noticing that I did not pay much attention to his suggestion, he went on to explain,

'Perhaps you do not realize that in Spain it is the custom for anyone who has a church bell recast to have his name engraved around the rim and it is said that each time the bell tolls, it is asking for blessings from Heaven for that family. Probably Luis' ancestors had that very bell placed there and who but you have the obligation of restoring it?'

Old Padre Remigio rubbed his hands and nodded in approval as he listened to Peps' words.

'Indeed, Señor Marqués, it would be a great honour for the Señora Condesa to repair our church bell, and while she is about it a few nice new images sent down from Madrid would not hurt the devotion of my people either. Those old worn saints we have inside are so plain and ugly the townspeople cannot be expected to revere them.'

The 'plain and ugly' statues to which he referred were magnificent carved wood sixteenth-century pieces.

Adventures in Santa Marta

'Also we need an organ for this church. Nobody can keep tune without some sort of music to go by.'

I escaped into the church before Peps involved me in any more undertakings. But the bell of Santa Marta was soon in the back of our station wagon on its way to Madrid.

I had rather imagined that this little task could be taken care of quickly and that the bell would be back in the church ringing with a beautiful note within a short time. To my dismay I found it was a laborious procedure and also expensive. But the worst was yet to come. When the old priest saw that the new bell was smaller than the one that had been taken away, he protested loudly that we had robbed him of several pounds of ore. There was no way of making him understand that in melting down an old bell, a certain amount of shrinkage takes place.

Shortly afterwards, after spending two days at the *finca*, I remarked to my *guardesa*, 'How strange, Maria, not to have received the Padre's usual visit.'

That morning I heard a curious noise like a motor and as I looked out of the window, I saw a shiny new motor scooter encircled by waving black skirts winding its way down the hill. I could not believe my eyes. The world was certainly about to come to an end if Father Remigio had taken to riding a motor-cycle! I rushed down into the patio and arrived just in time to see a young priest lean his scooter against the stone wall and come to me with a smiling face and outstretched hand.

'I am Alonso Martin, the new priest of Santa Marta.'

As he spoke, I saw a line of fine strong white teeth. His skin was tanned and clean, his eyes were dark and friendly, the starched white collar under his black habit was immaculate, even his black shoes shone under their thin coat of dust.

'But what has happened to Padre Remigio?' I asked. 'I do hope the poor old man has not died.'

'Padre Remigio has been sent to the old people's home in Trujillo. I have inherited his house and I must say I do not know how the old priest lived at all in such a shambles.'

He did not know, but I did, because I remembered Padre

The History of Pascualete

Remigio's old housekeeper. A filthier old woman never existed. I dreaded her visits more than Padre Remigio's. Her toothless wrinkled face and her shrill-voiced chatter repelled me, and my only thought was to get rid of her as quickly as possible. Apart from delivering her master's message she was always anxious to line her own pocket. As soon as she had left, Maria, the *guardesa*, would appear as if by magic. Without a word of encouragement on my part she would open all the windows and take a broom and mop to each spot where the old witch had left her offensive odour.

'Don Alonso, I do hope that you have not also inherited the old priest's housekeeper?'

'Oh no, Señora Condesa, my mother and a younger sister have come to set up my house and they will find me a good housekeeper when they leave. In fact, I happened to arrive in Santa Marta the day that old woman left and it was quite a sight.'

He let out a boyish chuckle and continued to speak in a warm comfortable manner as if we had been chatting like this for years:

'Evidently she owned many cats, at least fifteen or so, and she refused to leave the village until she had them all tied into a sack on her old *burro*. The people in the village seemed delighted to see the last of her and were most co-operative in helping her round up her pets. But I did hear that when she arrived in the plaza in Trujillo, the sack fell open and the cats scattered throughout the town. They say the old woman almost went mad trying to find all her cats again.'

Santa Marta's new priest became as popular in Pascualete as he was with his congregation. We all looked forward to the buzz of his scooter as it bounced over our road. He would throw himself heart and soul into any activity which might be going on, be it a partridge shoot or hanging curtains. Priests in Spain are obliged to wear the ankle length religious habit at all times, but Don Alonso was very adept at wrapping his long clerical skirts around his waist to give him freedom to run or climb ladders.

One day on my way to Caceres I stopped in Santa Marta to pick up Don Alonso, who always found some parish errand which would enable him to take advantage of a trip to the city.

A view of
the bumpy
streets of
Santa Marta

Mules playing on the threshing field with a view of Pascualete in the background

Adventures in Santa Marta

This day he invited me to see his newly finished house. The little entrance hall was sparkling with its fresh whitewashed walls and each room, although quite bare of furniture, proved equally clean. In the little patio under an old lemon tree sat the mother and sister, busily crocheting.

We climbed the steep narrow stairway and entered a diminutive low-ceilinged room with one window and a table.

'This is my study,' Don Alonso proudly announced.

Only a new round black priest's hat of shiny thick velour with the classic broad flat brim lay on the table. There was not one pencil or piece of paper or book. But in the corner of the bare room on the floor I saw a pile of what appeared to be ancient manuscripts. I pounced upon them and took the top stack of yellowed papers to the window to view more closely.

'I found those papers, Señora Condesa, in a damp corner of the old priest's bedroom, buried in filth and falling apart from decay. They are obviously the archives of the church, but I cannot read the script.'

I turned the tattered pages which had been loosely sewn together in book form with thick yellow cord and noticed that those I had in my hand had been written in the fifteenth century.

'Don Alonso, these documents may provide new information about Pascualete, more perhaps than I would ever be able to find in the archives of Trujillo! I would like to take them home with me and study them.'

That night, even my increased knowledge of palaeography and my new magnifying glass were barely sufficient to decipher the old letters, completely blurred by time and Padre Remigio's careless treatment. However, I remembered that Padre Tena had a lamp which, when focused on old documents, brought out clearly in deep purple lettering the vanished words. The next day Padre Tena gave in to my pleadings and lent me his cherished quartz lamp.

In the beginning my enthusiasm was curbed by the boring births and deaths registered, but late one night as I was slowly unravelling a folio of old papers recorded in the year 1448, the quartz lamp brought out a name which gave me a thrill of excitement.

Yes, I was right! I could see it clearly now.

The name was Alonso de Loaisa. How could this be? A Loaisa in Pascualete more than a hundred years before Alvaro had bought the property?

I went on reading feverishly. It was maddening because the scraggly worn letters took so long to decipher. The document was a marriage contract between Alonso de Loaisa and Maria Sanchez de Torres. The dowry of the lady was long and tedious, but I read clearly that she was the owner of enormous properties which she contributed to the marriage. The names of each property were clearly recorded and among them was one called Pascual-Ruiz and another called Pascualete.

I studied the old papers until my eyes were burning and the next day I went to Padre Tena with my discovery. My friend picked up his magnifying glass which he held carefully between thumb and forefinger (the handle having long since disappeared) and scanned the tattered Santa Marta documents.

'Yes, *hija*, it is true. There were Loaisas in the region of Santa Marta before 1558. How strange! Why would Alvaro de Loaisa buy the property which should have been his by inheritance?'

The padre looked carefully at each ragged stack of papers which I had placed before him, and then he went on:

'If you could find more of these manuscripts we could discover perhaps how Maria Sanchez de Torres happened to come into possession of the tract of Santa Marta and exactly what relation Alvaro de Loaisa, who was born some forty-five years later, bore to her. It is almost impossible to solve the enigma of happenings so far back in time, but the archives of the old church will give you just the information you need.'

'That, padre, is impossible. Don Alonso has given me the only manuscripts in existence. The church archives must have been destroyed at one time or another and there are no others to be found. I had thought that, knowing the name of the owner of these properties in 1448, here in the archives we might be able to trace her ancestry and also her descendants.'

Padre Tena arose and walked into the next room, beckoning me to follow him. He pointed to the limitless shelves of yellow manuscripts.

'How happy I would be if I knew where to begin to look for this lady who lived in the fifteenth century! Undoubtedly the information we want lies in this room, but it would take more than a lifetime to read through all these pages of tedious script in order to find it. None of the manuscripts in this room have been catalogued. I have managed to catalogue one room of this size during my lifetime and the old archivist, Padre Naranjo, before me had also catalogued one room. But these manuscripts, I am afraid, will remain here waiting until after I have gone for the next one to take up the work. Old Padre Naranjo who died in 1926 was a much better archivist and historian than I and he might have been able to help us. He was the only man who has done any profound study of the ancient families of Trujillo, but alas! he is dead and gone.'

I remembered the two thick volumes of Padre Naranjo's history of Trujillo and its families which I had read carefully, not once but twice.

'But, Padre, I have read the only things Naranjo has published and I know he never mentioned anything about a woman by that name.'

'*Pues, hija*, do not despair; if God wishes He will enlighten you one day. It is not good for one to insist upon something when God does not feel the time is ripe.'

'Yes, Padre, but it is very difficult for me to leave this search just when it becomes both exciting and satisfying. Alonso de Loaisa's wife must have been the great-grandmother of Alvaro, and who knows where she got the property from? She was doubtless my husband's direct ancestor also. I must find out!'

Padre Tena looked at me with the familiar twinkle in his wise blue eyes.

'It is indeed extraordinary that the proof that Pascualete has been in your husband's family since the year 1558 does not seem ancient enough for an American to whom I had always thought anything over a hundred years old would be impressive!'

Padre Tena proved to be right. I had come to the end of a blind alley. Much as we searched, Don Alonso and I could not find one more manuscript of the ancient archives of Santa Marta. The young priest did discover a lot of papers that had belonged to old Padre Remigio. Most of them were bits of the old priest's weird poetry, but Don Alonso said he wanted to go over them carefully to be sure he threw away nothing of importance.

The next day on my way into Caceres, Don Alonso handed me a dirty envelope.

'This,' he said, 'contains a sermon which was delivered to the people of Santa Marta many years before by an important visiting priest and I thought you might be interested.'

He shook his head sadly and added,

'I made a last search in the church and among the old priest's papers, but not one more manuscript could I find.'

I opened the envelope and pulled out several tattered sheets of smeared purple type. I replaced them in the envelope, thinking to read the sermon, which undoubtedly was very boring, at a later date, and then stuck the envelope between the pages of a book and forgot about it.

11

A House with Buried Treasure

ONE DAY, as I was walking through the hills of Trujillo with an old tourist guide-book in hand, I came across the most extraordinary paragraph. Under a heading *La Casa de la Boveda*, which means the House of the Arch, I read:

'This thirteenth-century palace, property of the Conde de Torre Arias, is the oldest of all the palaces in Trujillo.'

I was startled. The last person to use the title of Conde de Torre Arias was Luis' grandfather who had been killed in 1936 at the beginning of the Civil War. I continued reading:

'It is located high up on a hill facing the Church of Santa Maria la Mayor. On one side is the convent of the Noble Ladies and on the other, the House of Pizarro. This *palacio* once formed a part of the ancient city wall of Trujillo and legend has it that there is buried treasure still undiscovered in this building.'

The book had obviously been written before the death of Luis' grandfather, but it was strange that neither Luis nor his sisters nor his uncle had inherited any property of this name in Trujillo. Nor had I ever seen it in all my wanderings around the city.

Retracing my footsteps, I climbed up the hill to the location mentioned. Yes, in front of me was the church. On one side was the convent, in ruins, and on the other side was the house of Pizarro, both on a much lower level than where I was standing. Behind me where the house should have been, was nothing but open country—a high mount of dirt with a few hovels where someone seemed to be living.

At the doorway of one of these hovels sat a woman nursing a child. Attracted by the beauty of the child, I went closer with the vague idea of chatting with the mother. But as I stood in front of the doorway, I looked up and there I saw the same *escudo* of the five roses! In fact, the entrance was very much like the arched stone doorways at Pascualete.

'But what is this *escudo* doing here?' I asked the woman, forgetting the usual amenities with which one always begins a conversation in Spain.

'Ah, Señora, there are many more of these down below.'

'Down below? What do you mean?'

Pointing to the ground, she said:

'Why below there are big rooms with columns and stairways and many more of these *escudos*. Of course, I have never been down there, as it is very dangerous, but my husband told me about it.'

The woman invited me into her one-room shack. It was almost dark, as no light entered except from the doorway covered with a piece of cloth to keep out flies. She walked over to a corner and lit a lamp.

'I will show the Señora where one descends,' she said and moved a couple of planks and a big stone. 'My husband keeps this covered up so the children will not fall down there.'

I saw nothing but an enormous black abyss and a few steps for descent. Curious, I asked, 'How long have you been living here? To whom does this house belong?'

'It belongs to the Conde de Torre Arias,' she replied.

'The Conde de Torre Arias? But he has been dead since 1936.' She looked surprised.

'Well, I don't know about that, but my mother was the *portera* of the Condes de Torre Arias and my grandmother before her and so I inherited this job when my mother died.'

'But, does anyone pay you?'

'No, but we have the right to live here,' and then she eyed me suspiciously and a look of fear came over her face.

'The Señora is not going to put me out, is she?'

'No, of course not,' I assured her, distressed to see her upset. 'It's just that my husband's grandfather was the Conde de Torre Arias, and naturally I am curious about this house.'

A House with Buried Treasure

'Ah, Señora, we have always been very loyal to the Conde de Torre Arias. Please do not put us out.'

Finally convincing her that this was the furthest thing from my mind, I wandered back outside and looked around me.

It now became clear that the entire hill upon which I was standing, overlooking the church, was a false level caused by centuries of debris. It dawned upon me that I had entered the little hut through a third floor window of what had once been the thirteenth-century palace of the Loaisas and that this house was none other than the Casa de la Boveda!

My first impulse was to go right back to that hut and descend into the black depths of the old palace. But the woman warned me that such a move would be most dangerous since the ceiling might cave in at any moment. She said that her husband had noticed that the ceilings of the rooms just below were cracked in many vital spots and he had not dared to go down for years.

I wandered back down the hill to the plaza, wondering what could have been the story of that house where the Loaisas had again left their mark. Obviously this had been Alvaro's city house and Pascualete was his country home. But the years had not been so kind to this home—and no wonder, for Trujillo has had a turbulent history.

Many civilizations were piled layer upon layer on those hills— beginning with the primitive Celtiberians and then later the Romans, the Visigoths, the Moors, and finally the Christian Spaniards of the last seven hundred years.

Deep in thought I arrived at Pillete's bar and took a seat at one of the outdoor tables. I must have had a pensive expression, for Pillete's first words were.

'The Señora Condesa is looking very preoccupied. Is something the matter?'

'No, not really,' I answered. 'It is just that wherever I turn I seem to find mysteries.' And I told him about the Casa de la Boveda and my discoveries of the morning.

'Pillete, you have lived in Trujillo all your life—can't you tell me anything about this house?'

'I wish I could help you, Señora Condesa, but I am not a very learned person. Of course, I do know that all those marvellous palaces on the hill were destroyed or badly damaged when the French were here. Look at this village! The French ruined it and we have never recovered from that.'

I knew, of course, that he was referring to Napoleon's devastation of Spain during the Peninsular Wars of 1808–1812.

'But Pillete, do you suppose there is a buried treasure?'

'Huh,' he snorted, 'you think when those French left here they left any treasure behind? *Que va*—they destroyed or plundered everything.'

'But perhaps it is the gold that some Conquistador hid away or maybe someone buried it when the French armies were advancing,' I ventured.

'It is because the Señora Condesa is an American that she is always so optimistic.'

I wasn't at all, but I longed for encouragement.

'Well, I know that those palaces have some wonderful stories,' said Pillete. 'I've been told that they were once part of the city wall. Back in the time of the Conquistadores, the noble families had the privilege of building houses on the city wall. And in return for this honour they had to take care of and defend—at their own expense—that part of the wall which bordered their houses. Of course, they had many, many servants who could fight in case of attack.'

'Perhaps the Casa de la Boveda was once just such a fortress palace,' I said.

'I would not know,' answered Pillete, 'but why does the Señora Condesa not ask Padre Tena?'

I took the guide-book to the good patient Father. 'Padre, the book says that this house dates from the thirteenth century. Do you think that is possible?'

'My child. I see no reason why not. In fact that is very logical. You see, it was in 1232 that the Moors finally were defeated by the Christians here in Trujillo. Many noble families and noble homes began at that period. For example the house of Tapia. Do

A House with Buried Treasure

you know how they got their famous *escudo* which you see all over Trujillo?'

I did not, but I could see that Padre Tena was determined to enlighten me.

'Imagine Condesa, the heathen Moors had been here for almost five hundred years, and they were fighting a desperate battle to the finish. There was a long siege and it was a particularly cold autumn and the Christian warriors were grouped together on the plains outside the city walls, suffering from cold and hunger since the Moors had completely cut off their supply line.

'The Christian captain—Tapia by name—seeing the situation desperate fell on his knees and prayed for help. And God heard his prayers and sent a great miracle. Clouds of ravens approached each carrying bread in its beak, which they dropped to the starving armies. So today the *escudo* of the House of Tapia always shows six ravens with bread in beak.'

I wanted to get back to my own problems, but Father Tena, once he started talking, was impatient of interruptions.

'And the Señora Condesa must have heard—as every school-boy in Trujillo has—the story of the great Mozarab who was the hero of this particular battle.'

'No, Padre, exactly what is a Mozarab?' I asked.

'The Mozarabs were inhabitants of Spain who, when the Moors invaded, remained in peace and harmony in the Moslem occupied areas. They learned the Arabic language and profited from their culture, but they always held fast to their Catholic faith.'

'This Mozarab,' the Padre continued, 'was called Fernan Ruiz, and he lived within the city walls. He managed to contact the Christian troops by covering himself with a goatskin and mixing in a herd of goats which were driven out of the city walls to pasture each day. And one night, completely unaided, he opened the gate which the Christians had decided was the easiest point for their attack, thus permitting the Christians to enter and capture the city.

The History of Pascualete

'That is why, Señora Condesa, every October 18 Trujillo has its annual fiesta in celebration of that "Day of Victory".'

Indeed, this was all very interesting, but I was preoccupied with the Casa de la Boveda and the buried treasure.

'But Padre, if you think the house could be thirteenth century, do you believe there could be treasure?'

'My child, I do not know,' he answered. 'The discovery of the New World brought great wealth to Trujillo. The majority of the conquistadores were from Estremadura and a large proportion were from Trujillo. Many of these young men never returned, but others came back and built magnificent palaces with their gold. Who knows what might have been hidden away?

'This was the peak of Trujillo's civilization. But in 1809 the city was ruined by Napoleon's armies and has remained much the same ever since. The most beautiful parts of the city, after the French sacking, became rubbish dumps and many ruined palaces became hovels for the poverty-stricken—just like the Casa de la Boveda.'

Alas, the old priest was not very encouraging, so I excused myself.

When I got back to Pascualete that evening, I could not wait to tell Luis. I showed him the guide-book and told him of the day's adventures.

'This is very strange,' he said. 'I am sure that when my grandparents' estates were finally settled there was no mention of a house in Trujillo. Probably as there is nothing there, visibly, no one sought to inquire as to the ownership of a vacant property. The next time we go to Trujillo we must check at the town hall.'

And so, with Pillete accompanying us, we arranged to check the records with the Mayor, and sure enough, the last entry for the property was the Conde de Torre Arias.

'Pillete, you must help us find that treasure,' I said.

But Luis interjected the sobering note:

'Aline, I have seen you through all your adventures and enjoyed your pleasure in them. But this time I am putting my foot down. If you have any idea of going down and exploring the buried parts of that house, I absolutely forbid it. You might easily be injured or killed. And if not you, then some man you hire to go down there. No. This is something that an experienced archeologist must undertake. One day, we will explore it, I promise you, but only when we can organize it properly.'

And so, my buried treasure still lies on that hillside, but I continue to hope that I might find it one day.

12

Another set of Relatives
—the Great Golfins

S o f a r, I knew that the original owners of our *finca* had
resided in Trujillo and in Pascualete, but I did not know how
it happened that we had inherited this property from Luis'
grandfather, whose family came from Caceres. Obviously a
descendant of the Trujillan family had married someone from
Caceres. But when? And who were they?

One day at lunch in Madrid with Luis' Aunt Carmen, a most
delightful and beautiful lady who is also an historical biographer,
I began to tell her of my struggles in discovering the history
of Pascualete. Carmen was immediately sympathetic to my
cause.

'I know that the family of Luis' grandfather, which was at one
time called Golfin, came from Caceres and that they were one of
the great families of Estremadura. Their house in Caceres, called
the Casa de los Golfines, is perhaps the most beautiful of all the
old fortress palaces in the country,' she said. 'I do not think that
you will be wasting your time if you try to discover something
about the Golfins the next time you go to your *finca*. Why don't
you visit a friend of mine in Caceres, called the Conde de
Canilleros, the greatest authority on Estremanian history in
Spain. You will be charmed by him because he is not only a
famous historian but he is a great gentleman, a man who was born
heir to the ancient Ovando family of Caceres. Since his youth he
has had an enormous affection for everything to do with history
and writing. He seldom has time for the world of society, but has
spent his life investigating all facets of Estremanian culture and
publishing valuable reports of his findings. His circle of intimates

includes the outstanding intellectuals in Spain today, all of whom hold him in the greatest esteem.'

Therefore during my next visit to the *finca* one hot day in August, I took the road to Caceres. I felt that Aunt Carmen's charms would at least assure me a reception by this eminent gentleman, but I was not at all confident that he would be tolerant of my amateurish questions about Estremanian history.

I drove through the impressive stone archway leading into the ancient part of the city. The tyres rubbed on either side of the kerb all the way up the narrow street, which ended in a handsome plaza with a Gothic cathedral forming the far side and three huge palaces enclosing the rest of the square. I approached the first person I saw and asked if he could tell me where the Conde de Canilleros lived, and he pointed towards the impressive granite structure directly in front of me.

On the magnificent façade of the Canilleros palace was the usual family *escudo*, carved in stone and situated just over the Romanesque arched doorway. The windows were covered by the intricately designed iron gratings so often found throughout Spain.

I went through the open doorway and climbed a few steps into a cool and refreshing patio surrounded by graceful columns and bright with flowers and green plants. In a few moments the doors giving on to the patio opened and a lean, distinguished man with a scholarly air and a warm smile approached. His well-tailored grey suit struck the only modern note in this typical sixteenth-century setting.

'I am Miguel Canilleros,' he said as he kissed my hand. 'Welcome to Caceres.'

He motioned to me to pass before him through the open double doorway and I found myself in a high-ceilinged library with railings on all sides and ladders leading up to second story bookshelves. There were several large writing tables, but we settled in a cosy corner with comfortable armchairs.

Spanish houses are usually dim inside. The huge outside shutters remain drawn all day long to protect the interior from the heat of the strong sun. The small infrequent windows in this fortress palace made the darkness even more profound and it was several moments before I noticed the many family portraits and illuminated genealogical charts crowding the wall space.

After answering my host's enquiries about *Tia* Carmen, I proceeded to explain my interest in the history of the Golfin family, desperately hoping that he was not going to find me an ignorant bore.

However, he offered me a cigarette and sat back in his chair, saying, 'Fortunately for me, you have come in the afternoon because, since I read and work until four in the morning, I never awake until one o'clock the next day. If you had come in the morning, my servants would not have dared to awaken me and I would have missed this delightful visit.'

By now I was accustomed and almost impervious to Spanish chivalry and the ease with which they pronounce the most exaggerated compliments, but this was still a reassuring introduction. He went on:

'How satisfying that finally a member of the great Golfin family is interested again in its glorious traditions!'

I felt about as much a member of the great Golfin family as I did of the Royal House of England, but I sensed that this was not the time to interrupt.

'I was born here in this palace, as were all my ancestors from the year 1511 when it was constructed by my forebears. Most of the old palaces of Caceres are still inhabited for certain parts of the year by the descendants of their original owners, but the Casa de los Golfines, the most beautiful of our palaces, has been uninhabited and neglected for the past seventy years.

'It is very nice to know that you, whose husband and sons are the heirs to the titles and traditions of the Golfins, will receive them with appreciation. For one who loves the wealth of history and who has dedicated his entire life to its study, as I have, anyone who shows an interest in these things I consider a close friend of mine.'

He looked at his watch.

Another set of Relatives—the Great Golfins

'It is almost six o'clock. My mother and I always have tea at this hour. Would you be kind enough to join us?'

We walked through the patio splattered with late afternoon shadows to the opposite side of the building, where an open door revealed a little old lady with sparkling white hair. She was dressed in black to the ankles, with a little narrow white lace band around her neck. I was introduced to the dowager condesa and we were seated at a small petticoated table to feast on thick black chocolate and soggy cognac-drenched cakes. I wondered why my hosts referred to this as tea and marvelled at the old lady's sturdy liver which had weathered so many afternoons of this typical Spanish repast.

My distinguished host and his mother began to make me gifts of fabulous forebears right and left as each centuries-old Golfin was dragged out of his tomb and discussed in the most intimate and gossipy manner. The role of impostor becoming each moment more uncomfortable, I tried now and then to put things in their proper place by making a remark about my *husband's* ancestors. But I could see that from now on I was a Golfin whether I liked it or not and I settled back to enjoy the sensation of belonging to such an illustrious family.

As I took my leave, I asked my host if he could direct me to the Casa de los Golfines since I had never seen it and I did not want to return to Madrid without knowing it. He looked at me in amazement:

'What! You have never seen the Casa de los Golfines? Nothing could be simpler—come with me!'

We took a few steps across the plaza, turned left at the corner of the cathedral and in that instant, right in front of me, I saw the most beautiful palace in Caceres. The last rays of the sun were lighting up the carved stone borders of the roof and the old stones of the fortress tower on the right-hand side glowed golden in the Estremanian sunset. As I looked down the façade I saw the careful lettering of an inscription carved deep in stone:

ESTA ES LA CASA DE LOS GOLFINES

The History of Pascualete

The Conde de Canilleros translated 'This is the House of the Golfines.'

'Since your husband's uncle, who owns the house, very rarely comes to Caceres, it is completely closed with only a caretaker and his wife to guard it. One day we must go through. The magnificent drawing-rooms and courtyards are well worth visiting.

'Before you leave we must take a stroll through some of these old streets. Caceres, as you see, is one of the few medieval cities which has remained undestroyed throughout the centuries.'

The narrow streets were like tunnels lined on either side by great granite mansions. There was a strong resemblance to Trujillo, but here there were no tumbledown buildings, no rubble to mark the passage of time. And each building had its own dramatic story which the Count related to me as we walked along. After our tour I drove home laden with pamphlets and books this charming man had given me.

'To think that it has taken an American to make the family Golfin come back to life!' were his parting words to me, and I realized that I had better get to work and learn something about their history before I dared set foot on the storied streets of Caceres again.

13

The Four Unfortunate Sisters

I N S P A N I S H the word *golfo* is used to describe a little scoundrel or ragamuffin and it is possible that this word originated with the family Golfin.

It does not surprise me, for as I began translating the manuscripts of the Caceres archives and reading the rare out-of-print books the Conde de Canilleros lent me from his library, I learned that the Golfin origins were indeed colourful enough to warrant contributing this word to the Spanish vocabulary.

They began as a band of French warriors called Delfin who came to Spain in the tenth century to fight against the Arabs. At the same time they fought the Christian inhabitants as well and for the next three hundred years they terrorized the people of Trujillo and Caceres. In the beginning they elected a king from their own ranks who then founded a dynasty. Towards the end of the thirteenth century a young king Alfon Golfin married the daughter of the mayor of Caceres and from then on his tribe settled down and submitted to the Spanish monarchy. It was Alfon who built the famous Casa de los Golfines which the Conde de Canilleros had shown me.

I managed to trace his ancestors down successive generations through the fifteenth century to one Sancho de Golfin, but there my information ended (see appendix C).

I might have left the Golfins right there at the end of the fifteenth century if it had not been for a call from the Conde de Canilleros one day several months later. He was spending a week in Madrid and invited me to join him at a literary meeting.

As I pulled up before his apartment in Madrid the following day I saw him waiting at the doorway with a chubby elderly man with thick black glasses whom I recognized as José Maria Cossio, one of Spain's most popular intellectuals. Neither was able to open the temperamental door of the jeep and I had to jump out and run around to the other side to let them in. I was fully aware that in a country where ladies do not struggle for themselves, and where gentlemen do not even carry packages this was practically a *faux pas*.

However, with my dignified passengers squeezed close up beside me, in my excitement I wound through the traffic, red lights and all, to the address the Conde de Canilleros mentioned, and parked in front of a fire hydrant, which was the only empty spot on the street. On alighting my companions looked as if they might consider more carefully any future rides with American women drivers!

The literary meeting was held in a café which turned out to be just opposite my dressmaker, although I had never noticed it before. It was a typical obscure little café with many tables on the sidewalk in front. Ladies seldom go into cafés in Spain, but as this gathering was of an intellectual nature, my going had met with Luis' approval. Furthermore, I had rather imagined that after one visit I would either not wish to return or would not be invited.

I liked the old-fashioned atmosphere of the plain bar with its group of men in darkened corners, engulfed in smoke and surrounded by coffee cups. As we approached a far corner some elderly priests and scholars rose to their feet and I was carefully introduced to each, with much bowing and hand kissing.

This meeting was what is known in Spain as a *tertulia*, the Spanish word for any group of people who meet periodically to exchange opinions. In olden times, which in Spain means almost any period before the Spanish Civil War of 1936, practically every Spanish man had his *tertulia*. Since the Civil War this custom has lost much of its popularity, and most of the men who continue the practice are generally of an older generation.

When my companions politely inquired what I was writing, I began to feel a bit uncomfortable. Fortunately, before I had a chance to reply, the Conde de Canilleros startled me by explaining

The Four Unfortunate Sisters

that I was working on an investigation concerning the family Golfin, which would be published soon. I turned to the Conde and in the lowest possible voice confessed that I had written not one word of my proposed family history.

'Well,' he said, 'it is a pity, but you must get busy and write up what you have discovered and publish it.'

I sheepishly confessed that I was at a complete standstill because I had not been able to find any more information after Sancho de Golfin. The Conde called out to a pleasant-faced man with lots of pens in his breast pocket, who he quickly informed me was Antonio Rodriguez Monino, Spain's leading bibliographer.

'Antonio, what's the best source of Golfin history?' This began a long exchange of notes and papers which would supply me with the necessary information. And so with the aid of my *tertulia* friends I went on piecing the Golfin story together.

To each new generation after Sancho, sons had been born, and thus the name of Golfin continued illustrious for many centuries in the history of Estremadura. However, in the nineteenth century for the first time since 1260 the heir to the family had no son and the great name of Golfin was lost.

The last of the Golfins was born in 1760 in Caceres and was named Pedro Cayetano Golfin y Colon. He was an only son and therefore the sole heir to the Golfin fortune, which in 1788 he enlarged by marrying the only child of a noble Trujillan family, called Maria de las Casa y Mendoza, Marquésa de Santa Marta, heir and descendant of the owners of Pascualete. This marriage united vast tracts of land in the provinces of Caceres and Badajoz.

Since Don Cayetano's father was still alive when he married, he had not yet inherited the family title of Torre Arias and he began his married life using his wife's title which they continued to use throughout their lives.

Four beautiful daughters were born to this couple. In 1806 the eldest daughter, who was then seventeen, married the son of a Caceres family, at that time Spanish Ambassador in London. Don Cayetano, her father, prepared a fabulous wedding feast to which the entire population of Caceres was invited and which lasted for seven days. An enormous fountain of wine was set up on the plaza in front of the Casa de los Golfines and there were bullfights and dancing in the streets daily. And every night the old palace reverberated with the sounds of theatrical representations, balls and galas.

However, tragedy was not far off. A year later, word arrived from London that this daughter had died in childbirth.

Two years later the newly-married second daughter and her child also died in the same manner. The family doctors held a consultation and advised Don Cayetano and his wife that it was very possible all four sisters had some physical malformation and that it was improbable any could hope to give birth to an heir to the family.

As is often the case, sorrows never come singly, and a few months later the city of Caceres was threatened by the advancing French troops who had already broken through the ancient walls of Trujillo where they were reducing to rubble that dignified old fortress town, slaughtering its inhabitants and looting everything of value.

Don Cayetano, who was now a man of forty-eight, respected by his fellow citizens and looked upon as their leader and protector, was obliged to put his personal sorrow aside and to find a way of saving the people and the city of Caceres from destruction. It was useless for Caceres to attempt to defend itself against the invasion of the seasoned French army. It was also difficult to expect mercy from Napoleon's troops if they were allowed to enter the town without opposition, for all the Spanish cities hitherto occupied had been sacked heedlessly.

Don Cayetano decided to employ the only means in his power to prevent Napoleon's armies from destroying the city. He directed the citizens to remain within their fortress walls and to close the four great entrance gates, while he set out alone on horseback to meet the advancing enemy troops. Within sight of the populace looking over the powerful city walls Don Cayetano advanced to meet the officer in charge of the marching columns of men. Both stopped. They saluted each other. Five minutes later the people of Caceres, peering from behind the stone battlements, were astonished to see their Marqués de Santa Marta in company with three French officers turning their horses towards the city gates.

The four men entered a silent city and rode up to the door of the Casa de los Golfines, while the troops remained outside the town walls.

That day, by the time the three French officers left, Don Cayetano had been able to make an agreement by which Caceres became one of the few cities in the wake of Napoleon's troops to avoid all contact and destruction from them. Not one French soldier ever set foot in the city, and in return the Marqués de Santa Marta, at his own expense, gave supplies and money to maintain the French garrisons in Trujillo. Don Cayetano even became friendly with the enemy officers, who often came from Trujillo to dine at the house of the Golfins.

However, the French troops had already arrived at the little town of Santa Marta, whose poor buildings had crumbled easily before their fury, and the town was now so destroyed that of its two hundred families, only sixteen remained to eke out an existence and to rebuild their village.

All that was left of the pre-French period in Santa Marta were parts of the church and the *rollo*, a stone pillar marking the foundation of a new village, which had been placed in the main square.

Probably owing to Don Cayetano's influence with the French officers, or perhaps because of the fact that Pascualete was far from any highway, the French did not touch the old house, and it was there that the Marquésa retired with her two remaining daughters to live out the French occupation.

From my studies I deduced that the last member of the family to live at Pascualete was this Marquésa de Santa Marta, and therefore, over one hundred and forty years had passed until the day that Luis and I first set foot there.

When the French soldiers withdrew two years later, the

The History of Pascualete

Marquéses de Santa Marta learned that their palace in Trujillo had been completely destroyed. I believe that this must have been the Casa de la Boveda. The documents said that every piece of furniture, painting and article of value had been burned or pilfered. The Marquésa, who had returned to her old home each time she gave birth, and who had cared for the house of her parents lovingly since their death, never set foot in Trujillo again.

The death of his wife shortly after the return of the Spanish king to the throne affected Don Cayetano greatly and from that time on he lived very quietly. Several times his two remaining daughters wished to marry, but they always encountered their father's opposition.

In 1822 Don Cayetano, at the age of sixty-two and beloved by all who knew him, died in Caceres. Four years later the third daughter married and a year after, fulfilled the fatal prophecies of the doctors when she died in childbirth.

The youngest daughter, called Petra, remained the only Golfin heir and in 1832, at the age of thirty-four, she finally fell so desperately in love with a handsome young man called Jorge Gordon that she was willing to defy her fate and to marry. When the time came for her to give birth, she was brought to Madrid where the greatest European specialists were to care for her. The poor girl was three days in labour and finally died, after the most excruciating suffering, completely mutilated by the doctors' attempts to bring alive into the world her daughter, my husband's great-grandmother.

This only issue of the four Golfin sisters, Maria de la Concepción Gordon y Golfin, married in 1856 Don Enrique Perez de Guzman el Bueno, from Cordova, and this couple moved to Madrid where they made their home from then on.

The son and heir of Don Enrique and his Golfin wife was Luis' grandfather. He, in turn, had three children: the eldest, Luis' Uncle Alfonso, today carries the titles of the family; another son, Narciso, died at the age of twenty-five, unmarried, in Africa during the Spanish-Moroccan wars; and Luis' mother, Maria de la Concepción, was killed in an automobile accident at the age of

The Four Unfortunate Sisters

thirty-one. She had three children—my husband, Luis, and his two sisters.

After reading so much of the history of this family and of Estremadura, I began to have some understanding of why so many of the noble families abandoned these provincial towns. After the French invasion many were left destitute and their properties destroyed. It was not because they suddenly lost interest in the country that they moved to Madrid, but rather that life had come to a standstill in these areas—not only were homes and farm buildings demolished but also roads and bridges. And once more law and order ceased to exist and bandits took over. At the same time landowners were assessed enormous new taxes which added to their difficulties in rebuilding and reclaiming the ravished land. And so this move to the capital, which began as an interim means to weather the post-war era, with time became a general trend and these noble families became more and more isolated from their provincial properties.

In my research I learned that my husband's great-grandfather had parted with a sizeable portion of his property in 1873 when there was an attempt to bring a republic to Spain. Strangely enough, the Marqués de Santa Marta of that time, the Cordoban husband of the only child of the four ill-fated sisters, despite being of the nobility, was not only interested in this cause but gave large amounts of money to finance it. It was said that he could go on horseback from Trujillo to Portugal without ever going off his own property, but he afterwards sold great tracts of this land to obtain money to further the cause of the republic. After the downfall of the shattered republic the king of Spain removed the grandeeship from the title of Santa Marta owing to this Marqués de Santa Marta's republican activities. For many years the family reverted to using the title of Torre Arias which sounded less harshly in the ears of Spain's monarchists.

14

The Riddle of Pascualete

ANOTHER YEAR passed while I occupied myself with the Golfin story. This answered many more questions for me about Pascualete, but still there were big gaps I wanted to fill.

One day in Madrid, I was carrying an unbalanced stack of books from my bedside table to a niche in the wall when they crashed to the floor and several pieces of paper and old notes were scattered about the room. As I bent down to retrieve the books, a bulging dirty envelope caught my eye. For a moment I could not recall where I had seen it before, and then I remembered the day, over a year ago, when Don Alonso handed it to me.

'Poor Don Alonso!' I thought. 'Always trying to be helpful.' I had completely forgotten about his envelope and should have returned it long ago. Perhaps he wanted it back and had been too shy to ask me. I removed the crumbling typewritten sheets from the envelope and glanced over the blurred blue print.

It was dated 1923 and obviously some sort of sermon for it began:

'The theme of my sermon this day of the Feast of Saint Martha is "Work is only honourable, meritorious and ennobling when it is informed by Christian faith."'

I had decided to read no further and turned the page over when by chance at the end of the document I saw a familiar signature—Fray Clodoaldo Naranjo, the only real historian Trujillo ever produced. Because I had read many of Father Naranjo's books, I went back to reading the sermon.

'Therefore, in speaking to a hard-working religious farming village as this, I find it fitting to describe in broad outline the history of your town, the reason for its foundation and something about the family who founded it and who maintained their feudal rights until Santa Marta was converted in the eighteenth century into a Marquisate which today figures among the most distinguished of our aristocratic houses.'

As I read this second paragraph, I knew that this sermon was meant for me as well as the townspeople of Santa Marta. He was talking about our family! I was beginning to tremble with excitement and my heart beat faster, for perhaps this would be another clue to Pascualete.

'It all began,' wrote Father Naranjo, 'with a brave and noble man who lived in Trujillo during the Arab domination. His name was Fernan Ruiz Altamirano. Through him the Christians were able to take the city of Trujillo from the Moors in 1232. When the newly conquered lands were divided among those nobles who had secured the city's freedom, Fernan Ruiz was awarded the most choice lands of the region, which were precisely these beautiful rolling fields and green oak groves surrounding this village of Santa Marta.

'These rich farm lands in due course were inherited by Fernan's grandson, Pascual Ruiz, who built Pascualete, the first country house in the district, and who founded there a prosperous farming settlement. I think there is no one in this village who is not familiar with that old palace.'

I stopped. What a blind idiot I had been. Why had it never occurred to me that Fernan Ruiz, the hero of Trujillo's liberation from the Moors, was none other than the grandfather of Pascual Ruiz? Of course, the name Ruiz was as common as Smith is in America, but just the same, it should have occurred to me. So at last I knew when and how Pascualete had begun!

I continued reading: 'From Pascual Ruiz these lands passed down to a great-granddaughter called Maria Sanchez de Torres. She was a lady of great elegance and in 1438 she married a military officer, descendant of the Royal House of France, called Don Alonso de Loaisa.'

So this was the link between the Ruiz family and their descendants and my Loaisas.

The History of Pascualete

'It was this noble couple,' Father Naranjo continued, 'who established a village not far from their fortress palace of Pascualete for the inhabitants of their lands. Don Alonso and Doña Maria, in order to encourage their vassals to be honourable and hardworking, at the same time built a fine church to satisfy the spiritual needs of their people. Our poor church today is a far cry from what it was then, because many centuries later Napoleon's troops destroyed and ruined everything of value in this village.

'The descendants of this same family in those days were called the Marquéses de Santa Marta and they restored the parish church, but because of the chaos of the moment they were obliged to do so modestly and without artistic pretensions.

'The sample of piety which this family always gave to their dependants lives on in this simple church and in the yearly Candlemas celebration which Doña Maria de Torres initiated four hundred years ago. Their charity towards the village and their example of Christian democracy was rewarded by God when the family name was ennobled by a saintly son, Fray Jeronimo Loaisa, first Archbishop of Lima, in Peru. Although the Marquéses de Santa Marta for many years have not set foot in their ancient feudal lands one day they will return. And may they find the village their ancestors founded so long ago a living testimony of these same virtues of piety, charity and Christian democracy.

'I say to you in closing, good people of this village, do not lose the spirit for which you were placed under the care of Saint Martha and do not lose sight of the noble ties of your village. Work with faith. Our Lord Jesus Christ knows how to reward those who work with faith.'

As I came to the end of the sermon I wanted to scream, to shout. It was too good to be true! As Padre Tena had cautioned me, the ways of God indeed are strange. This Father Naranjo, some thirty years ago, wrote this message that one day I might find it and understand its meaning. Pascualete had been in Luis' family since 1232—over seven hundred years!

Escudo of Pascualete which is found over the main door

The view of the countryside from
the Church of Santa Marta

The Riddle of Pascualete

And here I had been consuming the archives of the entire province for more than a year when I had the key to the mystery of Pascualete in several sheets of easy modern print.

Now I could remember Juan, the *arrendatario*, once mentioning that old Father Naranjo often used to stop at Pascualete on his way to Santa Marta to say Mass. Juan then was a young man, but he remembered clearly and even with warmth the aged priest who was so fascinated by the old stone building.

'It is strange, Señora Condesa,' Juan had said, 'how the kind old *cura* would wander from one room to another, tapping around with his walking stick and copying carefully in his book the designs on the old *escudos*.'

The very next morning I ignored all my plans for the day and grabbed the car to make the trip to Trujillo. So many things were making sense in my head on the way. So all the people who had lived in our old house were related! I had been more than right about Pascual Ruiz. And that wonderful little character, Fernan Ruiz, who crept out of the city of Trujillo covered in a goatskin, defying the hazards of a bitter battle. Now I realized the *escudo* of the five roses must have been placed by Alonso de Loaisa and not Alvaro.

But there were still gaps to fill in. Who were all the other people through whom the property had passed in order to reach us? And I must verify all this information. Naranjo's sermon was probably a short résumé of what he intended to tell the people of the village that day. But he certainly must have had a reliable source for his tale. There must be manuscripts in Trujillo recording each detail.

Just about noon I pulled up in front of the old palace which housed the town archives. I rushed up the steps fearing that Father Tena would already have left his studies but when I reached the top there he was as usual next to the window, bent over a pile of manuscripts.

'Padre, come with me to the room Father Naranjo catalogued. The answer to all my questions is there, I am sure! Naranjo knew the whole story of Pascualete. He must have studied its succession for many years because it goes back to 1232. Imagine, Padre, 1232!'

I did not give my old friend time to speak nor did I have the patience to tell him the full story of what I had discovered. I dragged him into the room which held Father Naranjo's work.

'Now listen, *hija,*' said the old padre, 'I have looked in the catalogue Father Naranjo left and I did not find a mention of Pascualete or a Loaisa.'

'Padre, what would you say were the last manuscripts filed away by Naranjo before he died? Or at least the manuscripts he might have been working upon during those last years?'

'On that lower shelf in the corner is a stack of papers which Father Naranjo had been studying during the last years of his life, but those papers are filed under the succession of a branch of the Ruiz Altamirano family. They will have nothing to do with your Loaisas.'

I had already reached the papers and was piling one manuscript after another in my arms, to take into the adjoining room. Padre Tena's voice had stopped all of a sudden. He was at my elbow and I could hear him begin to speak again faster and with a new excitement in his voice:

'Ah, now I understand. You have discovered that the succession of the family Ruiz becomes Loaisa later on. How were you ever able to discover that?'

We spent the rest of the day poring over the succession of Fernan Ruiz Altamirano. I read that the first Loaisa to come to Trujillo was Alonso in the beginning of the fifteenth century. He arrived in Spain from France with two brothers, one Garcia, who became the founder of his line in Talavera de la Reina and another, Alvaro, who founded a house in Plasencia.

But it was Alonso who married the heiress to the Ruiz fortune and their son Francisco inherited from them the town of Santa Marta and the surrounding lands.

Francisco had a son called Pedro and this man was the father of my friend Alvaro de Loaisa. However, I still could not understand why it was that in 1558 Alvaro de Loaisa had bought

The Riddle of Pascualete

the lands of Santa Marta. After all, that was my first historical discovery and it stuck in my mind.

But going over the papers with Padre Tena I was at last able to clear up the mystery.

'You see, *hija*,' he explained, 'in that first book we read the author had obviously made a mistake, as often happens with historians. Now we can see from these documents that Alvaro certainly did not buy property he already owned in 1558. He had inherited it from his father, grandfather and great-grandfather. But what happened was that the King, who needed money so desperately, had offered for sale the inhabitants or serfs. This was like a big head tax or property tax which Alvaro paid and he acquired the civil and jurisdictional rights of the property which he already owned. Thus he was made the Lord, or Señor, over these people and was obliged to care for their needs and administer justice.

'Santa Marta then became a "Village Exempt", which means exempt from more taxes, and Alvaro de Loaisa ordered to be placed in the plaza a classic stone pillar, or *rollo*, bearing his coat of arms, to designate his señorio.'

The old records had answered all my questions. I learned that Alvaro married a lady called Doña Maria Portocarrero and the succession continued as follows:

Pedro, a son, who in turn had two daughters: Antonia, who died without issue and Maria, who became a nun in Trujillo. At her death the lands and property were claimed by a cousin,

Francisco Herrera y Loaisa, also a direct descendant of Don Alonso and Doña Maria.

Don Blas Herrera y Loaisa, came next and he had a son,

Don José, who served his king well as a general* in the navy and as a reward the king raised his señorio to a marquisate. He had no descendants, so the title of Marqués de Santa Marta passed on to his sister,

Doña Juana de Herrera y Loaisa, who married Don José de las

* In this period the rank of General was used in the Spanish Navy.

Casas. (Here the surname of Loaisa was lost after three hundred years.) This couple had a son,

Don Antonio de las Casas, followed by

Don Vincente de las Casas, who married Doña Rosa de Mendoza, Condesa de Quintanilla, and became the father of

Doña Maria de las Casas, who inherited both titles of Marquesa de Santa Marta and Condesa de Quintanilla. This lady, in 1776, married Don Pedro Cayetano Golfin, Conde de Torre Arias. Their only issue was

Doña Petra, whose only child also was a daughter,

Doña Maria, Marquesa de Santa Marta, who married Don Enrique Perez de Guzman el Bueno. The title was then passed on to their eldest son,

Don Alfonso, the Marqués de Santa Marta, Conde de Torre Arias.

Here the succession which had been so carefully traced by the old historian Naranjo came to an end with Luis' grandfather who was then alive. It was better than I ever could have imagined. Pascualete had survived the ravages of nature and of man, tempests and wars and most cruel of all, neglect. But stubbornly she had resisted and had passed through twenty-three generations of the same family from 1232 down to us.

PART THREE

LIFE TODAY AT PASCUALETE

15

Life in the 'Choços'

WHEN LUIS' GREAT-GRANDMOTHER, the only child of the four doomed sisters, inherited the *finca* in the middle of the last century, the extent of the property was more or less the same as that held by Alvaro de Loaisa in 1558, but by the time Luis inherited his share of the original tract of Santa Marta, it had been reduced to a piece of about three thousand acres which was termed Pascualete. However, many of the *fincas* bordering ours belonged to second cousins and to his uncle, the present Marqués de Santa Marta.

We found Pascualete run probably in the same manner as it had been in Alvaro's time. It produces principally wheat and sheep and there are also some one hundred and fifty cows which are used mostly for ploughing, while their offspring are sold for meat. The land is still cultivated by wooden Roman-type ploughs drawn by two cows, and modern agricultural methods, despite my early attempts, are non-existent.

For centuries Estremanian shepherds have lived with their families in round straw huts called *choços*. And still today one finds the *choços* scattered at different points on the property. They are built very low and to enter one must creep through the door, while inside one can stand only in the centre of the hut. The floor is slate and in the middle burns the fire which provides heat in the winter and serves for cooking purposes all the year round. The beds, made of tree branches and broom bushes, form a ledge around the inside, and if the family is large, the *choço* is larger in order to accommodate more sleeping space.

The only concessions to the twentieth century which I ever saw in the *choços* were the inevitable alarm clock hanging on the straw wall surface and the farmer's calendar, which not only gives the days of the year, but also predicts in detail the weather. I often wondered who that genius was who prepared these little booklets. His predictions so often came true that rarely a wind storm or a drop of rain escaped his foretelling.

They have few possessions, these *chozo* dwellers, not only because they cannot afford them, but also they do not want to be bothered with too many belongings in a house which they move at least three times a year to accompany the sheep to different grazing areas.

For cooking, they use a long-handled frying pan and over the fire hangs a heavy wrought-iron chain with an adjustable hook to suspend the cooking pot at the desired distance from the flame. Any extra pots and pans are usually hung outside the '*chozo*' on a three-pronged stick driven into the ground.

Laundry is no problem for they take their belongings to the nearest river bank or to the well, where they wash and spread the things on the ground to bleach out in the strong sun. And children's laundry is kept at a minimum, since the little boys and girls alike are dressed in skirts with no panties or diapers until they are housebroken—quite a chilling sight in the winter to see the little tykes with their bare red bottoms exposed to the elements.

Once a week, the women of the *chozos* join together to make bread for the entire ranch in an ancient outside oven which probably has changed little since the days of the Romans. This small round stone building consists of one dark room with no windows.

The women stand at primitive benches and tables where they knead the dough and put the bread to rise. In a round dome-like oven the size of a small room they build an enormous fire with logs of *encina*, or evergreen oak, trees whose wood is extremely hard and produces an intense heat.

The oven has no chimney and once the fire has sufficiently heated the brick and stone walls, the women open the oven door and pull out all the ashes and remains of the fire. The smoke is suffocating since the only exit for the fumes is the one door and a small chimney in the middle of the room.

Life
on a *chozo*

Returning home with the water jug from the well

Life in the 'Choƶos'

I happened to be riding near by one day when suddenly the ancient wooden door swung open and out staggered what appeared to be two Indians on the warpath. But they were only Isidora, covered with streaks of white flour, tears and soot; and Antonia, choking and spluttering in the streams of smoke that gushed out with them.

When I asked why the chimney was not located in the roof of the oven, Isidora looked at me as if she were about to explain something to a five-year-old child.

'But Señora Condesita, the heat of the fire would escape with the smoke. This way the oven remains hot for many hours.'

Once the oven is clear of all debris and ashes, the women slide in the dough on long wooden planks. One would think that bread made under such primitive conditions and with such pains would have a delicious flavour, but I must confess that this heavy and rock-like bread is the worst I have ever tasted. However, the women insist that its unleavened flour is filling and healthy for a hard-working man.

In the spring and autumn, at the time when the baby goats are born, we often visited the *choƶo* of the goatherd. One evening as we were riding up the summit of the little hill, Juan, who was accompanying us, pointed to a cloud of dust made golden by the last rays of the sun, where a flock of sheep was moving to its night enclosure. As they went by the soft agreeable cadence of their bells greeted us.

Juan watched them for a few moments and then turned to me:

'I can understand anyone having a fondness for sheep; but goats, hugh,' he said contemptuously and pointed toward the *choƶo* at the top of the hill. 'Goats are the dumbest animals in creation. Why, their offspring are so stupid they are not able to follow their mothers until they are several months old, but the baby lambs, born during the day's pasturing, get up immediately and follow their mothers with no difficulty.'

As we arrived, the loud bleating of the baby goats bespoke their hunger and anxiety to join their mothers who were just returning from the day's grazing. Catalina, the goatherd, was just opening the door of the pen and out ran a stream of multicoloured little goats, each of whom with amazing facility searched out its mother from the herd and began to suck avidly.

Catalina's little eight-year-old grandson appeared with an old bucket and walked into the midst of the herd. With great efficiency he grasped the nearest goat by the hindleg and pulled the animal towards him. Then he placed the bucket between her two legs, squatted on his heels and began to pull expertly at the teats.

Meanwhile the few rams stood by with their long goatees wiggling back and forth as they chewed, some of them looking very much like distinguished members of the Académie Française.

Another favourite of the children was Pedro, the shepherd. One day I came across him lying on his back, his crook leaning against a giant encina tree and the flocks wandering seemingly unattended about him. When I chided him for his idleness, he jumped up.

'Oh, I do not have to worry, Señora Condesa. Old Leon does my work for me.'

He whistled and a large black shaggy beast came rushing at us, jumping all over his master and licking him profusely. Around his neck was an enormous iron collar studded with long spikes which gave him an air of ferocity not at all in keeping with his affection for Pedro.

'These dogs of Estremadura,' said Pedro, 'are the kindest and yet the most belligerent in the world and they have a history more noble than many humans. Why, there was a dog called Leon——'

The big black sheepdog, on hearing his name, jumped up again and this time nearly threw his master to the ground in his enthusiasm.

'No, no, Leon, I am not talking about you. I am talking about a dog like you who lived many, many years ago. His master called him Leoncico, just as I do you when you are very good.'

Pedro whistled Leon off to tend the flocks and I dismounted and settled myself on a slate rock, sensing that I was about to hear a story.

Life in the 'Choẓos'

'Leoncico was the dog of the great Conquistador Nuñez de Balboa who, by the way, lived in a town called Medellin not very far from here. Leoncico was a great dog in battle. He would grab the Indians firmly in his mouth and drag them unharmed to the Spaniards as long as the heathens did not resist; but if the poor devils made the slightest movement, Leoncico tore them to bits. This brave beast killed more Indians than any single soldier and it is said that ten men with him could accomplish more than twenty men without him.'

By now the sheep had left us far behind. In the distance I could see Leon whip in and out of the flock rounding up the stragglers. But the shepherd went on talking.

'The Señora Condesa might not believe it, but this dog became richer than most men. It was the custom for the booty captured after each battle to be divided equally amongst the soldiers. This booty was usually gold, precious stones and Indian slaves. Because of Leoncico's bravery the men decided that he should share the spoils equally with them and this became an accepted custom for fighting dogs in the New World.

'But the most magnificent thing about Leoncico was how he loved his master. When Nuñez de Balboa was unjustly imprisoned and sentenced to be beheaded, Leoncico refused all food and remained outside the barred windows of his master's cell until the last moment. The night of the execution the dog remained in the plaza howling up at the post which held his master's head and in the morning he disappeared, never to be seen again.'

*   *   *

When I first came to Pascualete, I used to feel very sorry for these people who had to live in *choẓos*. It seemed to me the saddest possible fate until the day when the young shepherd who lived in the *choẓo* nearest the big house, came to present his bride to me. I asked her how she liked her *choẓo* and if she would not prefer to live in one of the buildings around the patio.

Life Today at Pascualete

'Oh no, thank you Señora Condesa, my straw house is clean and smells so good, and it feels nice to be out on the plains and to hear the wind singing at night. Anyhow, my husband must be near the sheep, they cannot be left alone in the fields at night. The gipsies might steal some of the flock or a fox might come down from the hills to eat some of the young ones. We get up at five o'clock in the morning when my husband must go out with the sheep and then I have time to care for my old father-in-law, who is now like a baby since he cannot feed himself.'

'Do you mean to tell me that your father-in-law lives with you!' said I, remembering very clearly the close quarters of the little *chozo* where the bed was a narrow circular shelf around the interior.

'Yes, he is very old and there is no one else to care for him.'

It was very difficult to ask these proud, reticent people questions about their personal lives, but often my curiosity got the better of me. What amazed me most perhaps was how they ever managed to meet and marry anyone in the isolated country around Pascualete.

Maria, my *guardesa*, was one of the few persons I could ask, but even she was not easy to question and I had to lead into my subjects gently. One day I asked her how long she and Primitivo had been married.

'Fourteen years, if it please the Señora Condesa,' she replied, standing in front of me with her hands at her side. No wiggling, self-conscious woman was she!

'Maria, how did you meet Primitivo, since he has always lived on this farm isolated from the world?'

'Primitivo used to accompany his father to Sierra de Fuentes, where I lived, to buy stores and to shoe the horses now and then, and each year he came for our town feast day.'

Sierra de Fuentes, I knew, was a village eight kilometres on the other side of Santa Marta.

'Did he know your family?'

'No, but the feast of the patron saint sometimes lasts for several days and everyone joins in the gaiety. At night the town plaza is surrounded by stands where they sell water-melons and home-made cakes and hams. There is also a stand where places are raffled for the honour of carrying the Virgin during the procession the following day. A band comes all the way from Caceres to play for the nightly dancing in the street. There we would go with our mothers and fathers and the young men could ask us to dance. When I was eighteen I was allowed for the first time to join in the dancing and Primitivo was the first young man to ask me.'

'But when did he ask you to marry him.'

'Oh, he asked me to marry him right away,' she said, permitting herself a trace of a smile. 'But we had to wait seven years. People in our village do not get married until they have saved up enough money to pay for the new house and all their expenses for the following two years. And then the Civil War broke out and Primitivo was away for three years.'

Maria, who was always so extremely impersonal with me and everyone else, was obviously not enjoying this question and answer session, but I decided to press my luck or I might never get her to talk again.

'What about childbirth, Maria? Did you give birth to your children here on the farm?'

'No, although my mother-in-law did give birth to her children right here at Pascualete and although some of the women in the *chozos* do, I went back to Sierra de Fuentes.'

'Do the doctors in those small towns use anaesthetics or anything to ease the pain?'

'Oh no, Señora Condesa, most times there is no doctor at all but we do have a very good midwife.'

I knew that the care of the baby after birth for the first two years was quite simple, since the children received nothing except the mother's milk during all that time. In fact, it was sometimes quite terrifying to see strong-toothed two-year-olds munching away at their mother's breast. But at least this way the women avoid all the paraphernalia of sterilizing formulas and foods.

I also wondered where the people of the *chozos* were buried when they died, for throughout Spain burial must take place within twenty-four hours, probably because there is no embalming.

'No Estremanian would be caught dead in a *chozo*, Señora Condesa! That is a real disaster,' said Maria.

She appeared shaken by the very thought. I wondered why death in a *chozo* was more disastrous than any other place and she continued:

'They run the risk of being cut to pieces for the autopsy which is obligatory for persons dying without a doctor's certificate.'

This surprised me as I could not imagine autopsies being compulsory in these remote areas.

'Therefore, when the moment approaches, the dying person is put in a cart or on a *burro* and rushed to the nearest village. If he arrives in time a very grand and elaborate funeral wake will be celebrated where his friends and relatives will sit by his coffin all night long and mourn and cry as loudly as possible. Poor Paula's funeral was really beautiful. They had the best group of weepers Sierra de Fuentes had heard in a long time.'

I remembered very well poor Paula's death, for it was my introduction into the lengthy mourning customs in the country sections of Spain.

We arrived one day at Pascualete to find even the little four and five-year-old children dressed from head to foot in black. And my patio, normally so gay, was enveloped in gloom.

'What happened?' I inquired.

The children explained that Primitivo's niece, Paula, had died and everyone's clothes had been dipped in black dye. I realized that I would see nothing but black on children and grown ups for the next six months, for I was no longer foolish enough to think that I could have any effect on such established Spanish customs.

The next day, thinking it might cheer up Maria, I asked her to come to Trujillo with me to help with the shopping. While awaiting her in the jeep, I saw Primitivo and his son, José, appear in the patio carrying an enormous black chiffon cloth which they draped carefully upon Maria's head and shoulders. This black veil reached the ground and covered her face. I looked at the spectre who was to accompany me and suggested that perhaps that little extra touch of mourning was not necessary for just a shopping expedition.

'But, Señora Condesa,' Maria assured me, 'it would be a most irreverent reflection upon our late niece if I removed my veil.'

As she climbed in, the black shroud caught in the door and wound itself around us and all the way to Trujillo I was constantly disentangling myself from the swirling yards which threatened to blind me. In the car I asked her about Paula.

'A real tragedy, Señora Condesa! You surely remember young Paula, one of the brightest girls in the village and only twenty-seven years old?'

'But Maria, what could a young girl like that die from so suddenly?'

Maria continued to stare straight ahead at the open highway and blandly answered, 'Oh, she died of nerves.'

I had heard Maria say many strange things before but this time I was stumped.

'Maria, nobody ever dies of nerves. If people died of nerves, I would have been dead a long time ago. Think hard, her sickness must have had some other name.'

'Oh no, Señora Condesa, "nerves" is a very known disease in this part of the world. Suddenly one day she got so nervous that not even eight people could hold her down and then she just died.'

The next day as we were having lunch Luis, who had just returned from shooting with Primitivo and thirteen-year-old José, remarked that during the trip the little boy had had a very slight epileptic attack. Neither of us was aware of the fact that this child might be epileptic, and being very upset by this news I went to look for his mother.

I found Maria ironing. Her table was next to the window to get as much light as possible and she was unhooking the lid of a strange object shaped like a thick-bottomed flat iron but with a little chimney sprouting out behind. As she filled the iron with hot embers I questioned her.

'Maria, I want to talk to you about José. The Señor Conde told me that he appeared to be a little ill this morning.'

'Oh yes, I know. Primitivo told me that José got a bit dizzy and I must say he has had these attacks of "nerves" once or twice before.'

I realized now that 'nerves' was nothing else but epilepsy, and I determined that this youngster should not suffer the same fate as Paula.

'Now Maria, I do not want to frighten you, but I would like to take José back to Madrid with me and have some of our doctors look at him and cure these nerves.'

'Of course, if the Señora Condesa is willing, I will be more than happy. But I must warn the Señora Condesa that no one can do anything for "nerves", and one can only hope that José's will not be a serious case like Paula's.'

For the first time I saw fear in her eyes.

'If the Señora Condesa only knew what a worry this has been for me since José had his first attack.'

This, I think, was when I fully realized how little knowledge these people had of modern science and medicine, and I knew my responsibilities at Pascualete were only just beginning.

But their reactions to illness, health problems and the like, never ceased to amaze me. I remember especially one morning, when Maria brought in my breakfast tray, I noticed that tears were running down her face and she was making a great effort to hold back her sobs. When I asked what was the matter, she said:

'Ah, Señora Condesa, God has seen fit to send a great tragedy to my family.' I could see she did not want to discuss it further, but I insisted she tell me.

'Well, I do not like to trouble the Señora Condesa with sad news, but she will realize how I feel when I tell her that last night my sister gave birth to quadruplets—four children, Señora Condesa!'

'But, Maria, how perfectly wonderful. Why are you crying?

This is a moment of great rejoicing. Think what a rare thing has happened right in your family'

'But Señora Condesa, this is the worst thing that could befall my poor sister. Quadruplets mean four mouths to feed instead of one and they can barely feed the two children they already have.'

I could see she was desolate, so I offered to drive her into Caceres, where her sister had been taken to the Provincial hospital. Maria sobbed all the way to Caceres, and when we arrived I found that the rest of the family had taken this event in much the same manner.

The little babies looked strong and fit and the new mother was in good health, but inconsolable. The father was beyond assistance and the grandparents and various relatives could do no more than shake their heads sadly. When a photographer from the Madrid newspaper appeared to take a picture of the new mother, I thought perhaps they would begin to cheer up. I tried to convince them that many people would send money for the support of these babies, but they did not believe me.

We returned that afternoon to Pascualete and Maria retained her mood of depression until about a week later, when her sadness gave way to smiles.

'Si, Señora Condesa, God has heard our prayers. Two of the babies have died. You see God is good and saw the problem my poor sister would have trying to support four new mouths at the same time.'

To me, it was a sad blow, but the quads' family were sincerely happy, and with Maria calm again, joy and peace returned to Pascualete.

16

A Pascualete Wedding

ALTHOUGH PASCUALETE was cut off from the rest of the
world, it seemed to me a paradise. Whenever I could, I
escaped from Madrid and my other activities to this
enchanted world of great beauty and constant surprises, centuries
away from the rest of civilization.

At almost any time of year the sky over Estremadura seems to
be a deep blue arch that has nothing to do with the sky over other
parts of the world. It appears much lower and always gives me
the same feeling of snugness as a warm, well-protected house. At
night this ceiling is covered with stars whose constellations are
amazingly distinct, and in the daytime, the strong yellow sun
throws a warm light over everything it touches. When the grass
is green it appears more vivid than other grasses and when the
earth is barren it becomes a bright red and orange, sometimes
even yellow.

The clutter and complications of modern life had not yet come
to Pascualete. Strange noises of other worlds—radios, telephones,
newspapers, buses and trains—these were not known.

With modern commerce so far removed, one of the most
important events of the season was the arrival of the pedlar. He
made his rounds from one *finca* to another on a *burro* laden down
with bulging sacks or with a covered wagon from which he
unpacked a tempting assortment of ribbons, materials, sugar,
beans, knitted sweaters and knives. When he came to Pascualete
he usually drove right into the central patio and in no time the
women from all the *choços* appeared and began to chat gaily with
him as he slowly and dramatically unpacked and spread his goods
on the ground. I, too, welcomed his arrival, for often I found
myself in need of just one more spool of red thread or a bit more

white cotton to finish some curtain or bedspread, and even if that were not the case, I was just as tempted as the other women at Pascualete. And I enjoyed the bits of gossip and news he brought from the near-by *fincas*.

Not so welcome, but quite an event nonetheless, were the gipsies who from time to time passed through from Caceres on their way to the country fairs in Trujillo. Their main occupation at the fairs was horse and mule trading, at which they have long been experts. They were a decorative, but at the same time motley-looking crew. The men and women can be extremely handsome, with their dark skins, delicate features and snapping black eyes, but more often they were toothless and dirty. They rode beautiful horses and mules and usually arrived in a group of thirty or forty, with one or two mule-drawn covered wagons.

Many small children sat up in front of their parents on the animals, while others hopped and skipped behind. Even the little girls were dressed in bright-coloured, full-length skirts and wore dabs of lipstick and rouge.

Since I love Spanish gipsy music and dancing, I once made the great mistake of inviting a passing band of gipsies into the patio. They had claimed that they could all dance and sing very well, but I soon discovered that there are many gipsies who do not know how to do either. However, they managed to make an awful rumpus and afterwards when they were refused money for their disturbance, several old gipsies as they passed under the arch looked up at the moss-covered *escudo* above and shook their fists in a gipsy gesture of malediction.

After their departure we found that they had gone off with several chickens, two sheep, a couple of hams, somebody's horse saddle and a garden shovel, all in the space of fifteen minutes.

Social events around Estremadura were limited, but the most important function by far was a wedding. Our first invitation to a country wedding came from Juan, our *arrendatorio*, whose son Andres was soon to be married.

Andres was tall, dark, handsome and intelligent, and Juan often bragged that his son was the best farmer for his age in the entire area. Naturally, I took it for granted that Andres' *novia* or betrothed would be the prettiest girl in the province—since he obviously had his pick.

But one day Pepe set me straight about that. The bride-to-be was the only daughter of the man from La Cumbre who had made our dining table. This girl was considered quite an heiress in that region, and Juan had selected her to be his son's bride.

'Andres' *novia* pretty? Señora Condesa, she is the most ugly woman that I have seen in my life,' Pepe told me. 'And what is more, she is ten years older than Andres and does not have a single tooth in her head.'

It not only amazed me that Andres would agree to such a marriage, but indeed, was willing to court her for a period of four years. All along I hoped that some more attractive country lass would win Andres away from his intended, but it was explained to me that in Estremadura the oldest son was obliged to obey his father's orders and Andres, above all, was a good son.

The month for weddings is September, because it is the only time of year when the farmers have no work. The harvest is over and it is not yet time for ploughing and seeding the winter crops.

Luis and I were invited to the wedding months in advance and I realized that under no circumstances could we be absent from this event.

One hot sunny day in September we took the dusty road to La Cumbre and arrived just a few minutes after the bridal party had entered the church. When we decended from a large and impressive car—impressive because it was the only car that had ever been near the village of La Cumbre—the townspeople mobbed us. After a difficult struggle through the crowds we managed to get to the door of the church, where we were led to the front and seated with the bridegroom's family.

I found myself in a beautiful, cool, high-ceilinged fifteenth-century church, whose elegance and simplicity seemed to have nothing to do with the shabby stone and mud houses that comprised the rest of the village. I recognized Andres' strong broad shoulders, which already had the farmer's tired stoop. He was wearing a dinner-jacket, probably rented in Caceres for the occasion and certainly the only one ever seen in La Cumbre.

But my eyes, after a glance at Andres, remained riveted on his bride. She was very short, not even reaching Andres' shoulder, so that he was obliged to bend low when the moment came to place the ring on her finger. The skirt of her gown was of white satin and the bodice of lace. An enormous complicated bow rested on the ample *derrière* of the lady and the long train of her gown reached almost to my feet in the second pew. On her head was a white velvet hat encircled by a wreath of flowers made of something that looked like pipe cleaners and she carried a bouquet of chenille flowers.

When the bride turned around I had to admit that Pepe was right. The poor girl *was* ugly, with lots of very tightly-curled black hair, and when she smiled she revealed two lone teeth which were false and I later learned had been put in just for the wedding. However, she had two rapt admirers. Seated on a wooden bench to the side of the altar were two little girls with burnt brown country faces and damp yellow curls whose eyes followed her every movement, enthralled.

Juan, as *padrino* of the wedding, stood throughout the ceremony at the altar, painfully aware of his conspicuous role and looking most uncomfortable in his new shoes and unfamiliar tie. Every now and then he pulled out a great white handkerchief from his back pocket and mopped his brow.

The ceremony ended and the bridal party turned and marched to the vestry to sign the marriage register in a screeching symphony of squeaky new shoes.

By now it was noon and much hotter than when we had arrived. The heat and dust were almost suffocating as we left the church and proceeded to the house of the newly-weds. It was evidently the custom after country weddings for the newly-married couple to receive their guests in their new home.

We entered a small whitewashed house where the entire populace was scrupulously inspecting each item. The carefully made bed was open so one could admire the embroidered sheets, the hand-woven blankets and the lace-covered pillows. The open closet revealed the groom's new horse and donkey blankets which were hand-woven and most striking in design and colour.

In the red and white tiled sitting-room was a magnificent radio—the bride's present to the groom and a large and hideous statue of Christ—the groom's present to the bride.

On our way to the town hall we passed many bars, boisterous with the celebrations, and as we reached the plaza we saw the preparations for the typical wedding feast in a huge cauldron. Our closer inspection revealed a pig submerged—feet, ears, tail and all—in a liquid to which a few potatoes and odds and ends had been added. It gave us the shudders. But after struggling through enormous portions of this gruesome stew, we were finally invited to watch the band in the plaza where the wedding dance had begun.

The townsfolk were jumping and dancing and singing. I saw Pepe swing a local girl around at a good speed. I wondered where Pillete was; Candida was sitting at a table in the far corner of the room, probably wondering the same, because I could see her glancing worriedly in every direction.

A plate was put in the middle of the floor so that each man could throw in some coins for the privilege of dancing with the bride.

'The Señor Conde must go first,' everyone shouted.

As Luis approached the plate and put his hand in his pocket he discovered that he had not one cent on his person! It was considered bad luck to loan money for the purpose and Luis was not able to dance with the *novia*. He put on a convincing face of disappointment and everyone seemed to feel genuinely sorry for him.

We drank what we could of the home-made red wine our hosts pressed upon us and soon the heat of the day was forgotten and we joined in the dancing which seemed to consist mainly in making a circle and sort of snapping the whip. When we left that evening we were thoroughly exhausted but our energetic country friends danced the night through.

A Pascualete Wedding

This experience whetted my curiosity about country weddings and I discovered still more amusing details. Evidently around eight o'clock in the evening the bridal couple are escorted to their new home. There they are obliged to spend the first night amid the clamour and joking remarks of all the villagers who form a circle around the house and sing and scream the whole night through. If they are not a couple of ample means, they have to spend the first six days of marriage shut in there, and it is the custom never to leave the house during this period. The closest friend of the bride acts as liaison between themselves and the outer world, arranging for the arrival of fresh food and water daily. At the end of the six days it is considered respectable for the newly-married couple to leave their home and to mix with the world again. However, in the case of our friend the heiress and her groom, they were able to leave the next morning on a honeymoon trip to Madrid where they spent ten days.

Some months later I realized what a truly lavish affair Andres' wedding had been. We were giving a shooting party at Pascualete in honour of some American friends. They had just arrived from New York to Madrid and came by car to Estremadura, and this was their first trip to Spain.

As we drove through the town of Santa Marta on our way to the shoot we were held up a moment by a procession passing through the main road en route to the church.

'It looks like a wedding,' said one of our guests.

'No, it can't be. Look, the woman is wearing black.'

But it was a wedding. Walking on the arm of the groom, the bride wore a black dress and a black veil, and she carried some flowers in her hand which looked as if they had been made of old newspapers. The girl was very ugly with a short, squat figure and she was crying her eyes out.

The groom also wore black, a handsome and strong-looking man and he, on the contrary, was grinning and smiling at everyone.

'Why on earth is she crying,' I wondered. 'She is so lucky, ugly as she is to catch such a nice man.'

Life Today at Pascualete

We had to go on to the shoot, even though everyone wanted to stop and go to the wedding. We watched them disappear into the church, where Don Alonso had been waiting with his most pious face.

That evening Don Alonso joined us at Pascualete for dinner and immediately the guests begged me:

'Please, Aline, ask the priest why that girl wore black today.'

I translated the question.

'You see,' said Don Alonso, 'in towns like Santa Marta when they have to buy a new dress they prefer to buy a black one to be on the safe side. That way, if there is a death in the family they will have something appropriate to wear.'

'But why on earth was she crying?'

'Ah, poor girl,' Don Alonso shook his head. 'She had every reason to cry. First, you see, her husband is not a very young man. Not young for a husband.'

When I translated this to one guest—a recent bridegroom of sixty-five married to a woman of twenty-eight—he naturally said:

'Why, that boy was young enough to be my son. What does Don Alonso mean?'

I asked the priest how old the bridegroom was.

'All of thirty-three,' he said solemnly.

'And how old was the bride?'

'She was thirty-four.'

'But Don Alonso, how could she expect to marry a man younger than that?'

'Ah, but that is very old for a man to be a husband,' repeated Don Alonso, as if we should all understand. I could see we would get no further on this subject, so I asked why else the bride had been sad.

'Poor girl, she was crying because now that she is getting married she must go and live in the country,' he said.

When I translated this my friends shrieked. They had been to Africa, to Canada and to all sorts of wild and isolated places which seemed quite civilized compared to Pascualete.

A Pascualete Wedding

'But Don Alonso, my friends and I think Santa Marta and Pascualete are about as country as a place can be.'

'Señora Condesa, Santa Marta is a village, after all. And this poor girl must go and live in the Sierra where her husband is a *serrano*—a shepherd who guards the flocks during their summer pasturage in the mountains. It is very lonely there and she will miss her friends and family in the village.'

17

Primitivo comes to Madrid

AFTER PASCUALETE was made liveable and attractive, the contrast between the house and the people in the patio was much more noticeable—especially with Primitivo and Maria, who, we decided, could no longer go around in their ragged country clothes.

'Aline, you must do something about Primitivo,' Luis insisted. 'He is a *guarda jurado*—a sworn guard and is supposed to be in uniform. Surely you must have noticed that at all *fincas* in Spain the guards are dressed in uniforms.'

Indeed, I did remember how fine they usually looked in their brown uniforms with revers and cuffs of red, green or blue, depending on the colours of the family. They also wear a wide leather strap from shoulder to waist and in the middle is a big brass medallion on which is inscribed, 'Sworn Guard of——', whoever the owner of the property might be. Gold buttons with the coronet of the family, leather leggings and a broad-brimmed Andalusian type hat completed the picture.

When I told Maria of our plan she beamed.

'Of course, Primitivo has felt badly about not having a proper uniform like his father and grandfather had.' And she showed me a photograph of Primitivo's father in his uniform when he worked for Luis' grandfather. Using the photo as a model, we sent Primitivo to Caceres to a tailor.

Two weeks later he proudly appeared in the patio for my inspection, and I had to admit that he made a very handsome guard. But alas, after all this trouble, he rarely wore the uniform. He seemed so afraid of spoiling it that whenever he had any slightly dirty work to do, he removed it.

'Of course,' I reproached myself. 'How silly I am! Naturally, he needs two uniforms.' When I told Maria to order another one from Caceres, she was genuinely upset.

'But Señora Condesa, that is a terrible extravagance. I thought I had taken such good care of Primitivo's uniform that it would last for at least ten years. Is the Señora Condesa disappointed in the way I have cared for the uniform?'

When I assured her this was not the case, she then gloomily prophesied:

'God will punish us for such indulgences. Two uniforms, indeed!'

About this time Luis decided we needed some good riding horses at the ranch, and he bought a three-and-a-half-year-old black Arab mare named Chiquita, with the idea of schooling her in Madrid and then shipping her to the *finca*.

We sent Chiquita to the Madrid Country Club for training but the grooms there said she would undoubtedly be spoiled as soon as she had been a few months at the *finca* and ridden in the sloppy fashion of country people.

So it was that Luis suggested Primitivo should come to Madrid for a little schooling himself.

This was Primitivo's first time in Madrid except for a brief moment during the Civil War, and as it was an important event in any man's life, the entire population of Pascualete turned out to say good-bye to the voyager. For days Maria had prepared for this trip. What she prepared, I will never know, for I had never seen Primitivo in anything except his guard's uniform and his farmer's smock.

For his trip to Madrid, Primitivo wore neither. As he got into the jeep, I recognized he was wearing one of Luis' gayer old suits which I had given Primitivo long ago. He wore no tie, no collar and he seemed very self-conscious and ill-at-ease in this strange attire. But the people of Pascualete beamed and Maria packed him into the back of the jeep with a large cloth sack, its four corners tied together, which was his luggage for the trip.

He was greeted warmly by our servants in Madrid and quickly

installed in his quarters. The next day I drove him to the country club to begin his training.

'Now, Primitivo,' I explained. 'Out here I want you to learn how to comb and curry a horse. I expect you to learn all the details of grooming and in addition, they have new advanced theories about weighing out a horse's food and so forth.'

'But does the Señora Condesa think that Primitivo does not know how to take care of animals,' he said, trying to restrain his righteous indignation. My mule and my *burro* are the best cared for animals in Pascualete. And maybe I do not know about weighing out a horse's food, but I certainly know when a horse has had enough to eat.'

'Yes, I realize that, Primitivo, but you know that Chiquita is a very special, delicate mare and needs special handling. That is also why you are going to learn to ride her here.'

'Ride? Why, the Señora Condesa surely knows that I can ride anything under the sun.'

Although contemptuous of these newfangled city notions, Primitivo got through his first morning at the club without incident. As I brought him back to the house I told him:

'Now Primitivo, every morning you must go to the club around ten o'clock. Watch how we come back. You must take the street car which leaves from the house and it will take you to within a kilometre of the club.'

'If the Señora Condesa will allow me,' he answered, I would much prefer to walk to the stables. I do not trust these machines that go clanging along the streets. I never know when the doors are going to open and when they are going to close. I do not know when to get in or go out. No, no, if the Señora Condesa will permit me, I will walk.'

'Primitivo, that is more than five kilometres each way!'

'*Sí*, Señora Condesa. But that is nothing. A strong man like me does not mind a little walk in the morning. And it is far preferable to risking one's life on one of those modern inventions.'

The first indication I had that things were not going so well in the servants' quarters was from my maid, who brought me my breakfast tray looking very tired and wan.

'Primitivo is such a nice man, Señora Condesa, that I hate to complain,' the girl said, 'but you know he wakes up at four-thirty in the morning and walks about with his noisy boots, opening and shutting doors and waking us all. I think it upsets him to see us sleeping. He thinks we are oversleeping and that he must stir us around to get up and do the work of the Señores Condes. Please, would the Señora Condesa tell Primitivo that we have her permission to sleep until eight o'clock?'

Poor Primitivo found the central heating unbearable and he was bored. He did not know what to do with himself during the afternoon and evenings. I suggested that he go into downtown Madrid, but he was too frightened of the traffic and lights which he did not understand. Eventually, we suggested to Pepe, the chauffeur, that he take Primitivo for a night on the town. The next day, I asked Pepe how the evening went.

'Well, Señora Condesa, all I can say is that I hope I never have to go anywhere again with that country yokel. First of all, he put on his guard's uniform—boots, hat and all—and of course, everyone in the tram-car stared at him and one or two people asked if he were a guard in the park.'

'That's not so bad, Pepe. You really should be more tolerant.' I admonished.

'Señora Condesa, that is not the worst of it. Every time a girl appeared on the stage—and the Señora Condesa has heard that these girls are not fully attired—Primitivo got embarrassed and started shuffling his feet, making such a noise that everyone turned round to stare at us.'

It seems too, that Primitivo asked Pepe in a loud stage whisper, 'How can such a spectacle be permitted,' which caused the entire audience to roar.

But this did not deter Primitivo from wanting to go again, and for the remaining three weeks in Madrid he was asking permission to see all the musical comedies in town.

When Chiquita and Primitivo had finished their schooling,

we shipped them to Estremadura in a large truck. But Primitivo was opposed to this modern means of transporting a perfectly healthy horse.

'It would be much safer to ride the mare to Pascualete,' he insisted, not at all dismayed at the prospect of a one-hundred-and-seventy-five-mile ride. 'It might take a bit of time, but she would arrive in good condition.'

We sent her by truck but as it turned out, Primitivo was right. When we finally saw the mare again, she was covered with cuts and bruises and the trip almost lamed her.

After that, I rarely argued with Primitivo about anything to do with animals. But with Maria, I still tried to maintain a façade of knowledge.

Maria's greatest worry was spending a peseta and she filled entire rooms with things I had thrown out, saying that perhaps one day we would need them. She even ironed out the tissue papers my maid packed my clothes in when we came down from Madrid. So it was no surprise to me when one day she said:

'Really, if the Señores Condes are going to have so many house guests every week-end, then we must do something about the eggs. It is a shame the fortune we are spending on eggs.'

I had noticed that somehow we managed to consume around sixteen dozen eggs in a week-end, and agreed with her.

'What shall I do about it, Maria?'

'Well, the Señora Condesa could raise chickens of her own. And I will be able to help her tremendously, for if I do say so myself, I have a magic hand with chickens. Primitivo says it is something one is born with. You see how well my chickens are and how they produce!'

This seemed a wonderful idea to me and so once again I got out my agriculture books and planned a glamorous modern chicken coop to hold about one hundred laying chickens.

As I had to spend so much time in Madrid, most of this work had to be directed by mail. After returning to Madrid, I received the following letter from Maria, written for her by Primitivo in his laborious script:

Primitivo comes to Madrid

'My excellent Señora, of all my consideration, I take the pen in hand to communicate to the Señora Condesa that the house of the chickens is almost finished. It is indeed very pretty and the bricklayer says it is fine enough for people to live in. It gives me pain to inform the Señora Condesa that the bill for building this house is *una barbaridad*. I have refused to pay it, as it is 12,000 pesetas. I do not permit the money of the Señores Condes to be taken by thieves. I hope the children are well and Señor Conde enjoys good health.

Affectionate remembrances from she who has the honour to serve your Excellency, Your affectionate and Faithful Servant who kisses your hand.

Maria Maestre, Pascualete 10 February.'

Grudgingly, Maria was persuaded to pay the bill for 12,000 pesetas, plus another for 8,000 pesetas for the furnishings and materials. I told her to prepare for the arrival of some wonderful white laying chickens—100 in all—which I had ordered at the exorbitant price of 95 pesetas apiece. But I had heard that these chickens were famous for producing more eggs than ordinary ones. I explained to Maria that each of these chickens would have a metal number round its foot and from this she could record the number of eggs each chicken produced. But Maria was not impressed and several weeks later wrote again:

'My Excellent Señora, of all my consideration, I take the pen in hand to communicate to the Señora Condesa that the pretty white chickens arrived. They match very nicely the white house of the chickens. But it gives me much sadness to inform the Señora Condesa that many chickens have died. 22 in number. The veterinarian says that these are very delicate chickens and it is too cold for them. He also says that if the others are to survive they must have a special food and they must have placed many vaccines against the sickness . . .'

Affectionate remembrances, etc. Maria Maestre Pascualete
2 April.'

Life Today at Pascualete

Maria's letter was indeed a blow, but even after a bill from the vet for 5,000 pesetas for the vaccinations, vitamins and services, I was still undaunted. Indeed, I was told to send to France for a particular oyster shell which was supposed to be especially appetizing to these chickens and I wrote Maria detailed instructions as to the mixing of the food and the feeding of the chickens. Faithfully, Maria kept me posted on their progress:

'My Excellent Señora, etc. . . . We received the food and your instructions are followed very carefully. But we feel it is necessary to inform you that as of today only sixteen of the chickens are still with us. The doctor says it was the pneumonia. It is very strange indeed that they should all die so because my own chickens are very well this year and so far *Gracias a Dios* none have been ill. . . .'

Maria Maestre, Pascualete 7 October.'

Madrid
Feb. 6.

'Dear Maria,
You will be happy to know that I have bought another 100 chickens, but this time I have not made the same mistake. I will not send these until they are a little older and they will have all their vaccinations before they arrive. It was explained to me very carefully that the best laying chickens are the most delicate and that one must be prepared for a few disasters in the beginning. Let us hope we have better fortune this time etc. . . .

La Señora Condesa.'

'My Excellent Señora, etc. . . . I take the pen in hand to inform you that of the 50 surviving chickens we have managed to collect one dozen eggs. I knew this would give the Señora Condesa great pleasure. They are smaller in size than usual but this is just the beginning. If the Señora Condesa would not mind, perhaps these very elegant white chickens may have a happier and longer life if I could cross them with my own simple but strong chickens. Would the Señora Condesa permit me to try this? Affectionate Remembrances etc. . . .

Maria Maestre, Pascualete.'

Madrid

'Dear Maria,

I have discussed with all the experts about crossing the chickens and they advise against it, since our chickens are such a pure breed. However, the Señor Conde estimates that each of those dozen eggs we finally collected has cost him something like 6,000 pesetas apiece and he says not only do you have his permission to cross your chickens with mine, but that he ORDERS that it should be done instantly or he will end a ruined man. In fact, I have noticed that recently at the mere sight of an egg the Señor Conde becomes very upset, so I urge you, the next time we are at Pascualete, not to discuss the matter in front of him, and try and avoid serving eggs for a while please . . .

La Señora Condesa.'

'Excellent Señora, etc. . . . I take pen in hand to inform you that the chickens are laying very well. We have no illnesses. The cross between the Señora Condesa's white chickens and my own is the envy of all Santa Marta. Primitivo took 27 dozen eggs to sell to Don Federico last Saturday. I am sure the Señor Conde will be pleased. I hope that he will have his appetite back again as we have so many eggs God will punish us for not eating them. Your affectionate, etc.

Maria Maestre April 20.'

18

We build a Swimming Pool and an Airport

THE MOST talked about innovations we made at Pascualete were a swimming pool and an airport, but before these two were completed we had our share of adventures.

To build the swimming pool, we had to find more water, for already each new bathroom was lowering the only existing well considerably. Luis and I discussed the location of the new pool but he was very worried about the water shortage.

'You know, Aline, the only solution is to bring my father down here. He is wonderful with a divining rod.'

'Luis, are you joking?'

'My dear, I could not be more serious. My father is one of the best water-diviners in Spain. He has found water on all his *fincas* and a friend of his even had him go all the way to Valencia where he found water there. Why he found water in a factory we own in the middle of Madrid, where for some reason or other we needed water.'

I tried to picture my distinguished father-in-law, a true gentleman of the old school, practising the superstitions of ignorant country people. No, it was beyond imagination.

'With all due respect to your father, Luis, you can't expect me to go along with such foolishness.'

'No, no you will see. If there is water here father will find it.'

'But what kind of materials does he use?' I asked.

'Oh, he is not fussy—whatever he finds on hand.'

And so Luis persuaded his father to come for another visit. He wasted very little time after his arrival, obviously taking his mission very seriously. And Primitivo and Maria did not seem at all surprised when he asked her for two knitting needles.

'Now,' said Luis' father, 'I need a string to tie the two ends together.' With two ends in his hand and the points going outward, he tested them a moment, then stood in front of the house, looked up in the sky, looked to the left, then to the right, and I could see he was putting himself into some sort of trance.

Primitivo watched every movement transfixed, and I could tell he had not the slightest doubt as to the success of this method. Everyone was silent and it was all I could do not to laugh out loud.

My father-in-law stumbled along as if not sure of his footing. Every now and then I noticed that the needles jerked downwards. It occurred to me that this could have been the result of my father-in-law's encouragement rather than of any supernatural powers.

We walked around to the back of the house, through the gate into the garden and there he said, 'I am following a streak of water, where do you need the well?'

Luis told him he wanted it somewhere in the garden, if possible. He went on, his hands trembling and walking as if slightly drunk, closer and closer to the house. Within a half-metre of a corner of the house, he stopped.

'Here is your water,' he said. 'And it is not very deep either. At about eight metres.'

The spell was broken and everyone started shouting and jabbering at the same time.

'But how can it possibly be so close to the house?' I asked. 'If we dig the house will fall in.'

But Primitivo could only say, 'What great good luck the Señores Condes have. Indeed Pascualete is a fortunate *finca*.'

Luis and I were both sceptical, as this place was the highest and dryest spot in the area—just the opposite to where we thought water should be.

'Don't be silly, son,' my father-in-law said. 'There is your water.'

So two workmen set about digging through heavy slate. On our first trip back to Pascualete we found they had dug six feet and still no water.

'My father is certainly going to pay for this well,' Luis said grimly.

But by the next trip they had struck a gushing well of clear fresh water, and that day my American faith in mechanization and science suffered another serious setback.

And so we had our swimming pool, and of course many more house guests and parties. Among our favourite guests were Peps Merito and his vivacious wife, Graciela.

During one of their visits I saw Peps looking thoughtfully at a part of our grazing land which is on a slight rise about two hundred yards from the house.

'If you would just cut down a few trees at the far end of that field, you could have a perfectly good airstrip.'

'But Peps, what in the world would I do with an airstrip? I haven't an airplane and Luis hates them.'

'Well, it would certainly be a lot easier for Graciela and me to visit you, instead of flying to Caceres as we do and then having to send a car all the way up that bumpy road to pick us up. Anyhow, you are bound to have other friends who have small planes and it is always good to have an airstrip. Who knows one day there might be a plane just over this strip in need of an emergency landing field.'

'But Peps, that's the last thing in the world I would ever need here—and think of the difficulty and expense and all sorts of machines that must be needed.'

Of course, Peps knew that any sort of extravagant idea appealed to me enormously. And as a matter of fact, I already saw in my mind a neat little watchtower and a man waving flags back and forth as I had seen at other airports. But then I came back to reality.

'No, Peps, this really is too absurd an idea.'

'Believe me, Aline, the reason I mentioned this is because you have such a good natural airstrip. All you must do is paint a large white arrow pointing north on the roof of your house, put up a pole with an airsock and take off a few of those trees. Remove the boulders and fill in the ruts. Nothing simpler.'

We build a Swimming Pool and an Airport

This time I really would give the people of Pascualete something to talk about and, full of excitement, I summoned Primitivo.

'Primitivo, I have a new job to organize here and need many workmen. We are going to build an airport.'

'*Si*, Señora Condesa, and how many men would the Señora Condesa need?' replied Primitivo, his face impassive. I suppose by then he was so accustomed to my wild notions that he was no longer shockable. I was completely deflated.

Peps marked out the distance carefully with the aid of a few workmen who laid piles of stones at the far corners of the rectangle. He pointed out the trees that would have to be removed and gave further instructions about stones and ruts.

'And most important,' he explained, 'this area must be outlined with large whitewashed stones so that one can easily recognize the exact spot from the air.'

I asked Primitivo how long it would take to finish and he said that ten men working for about a month should do it.

'Well, get me twenty men and let's do it in fifteen days,' I said. Every day I made at least four inspection trips to urge them along. I managed to rush them so that on the eighth day I was able to send a message to Madrid that all was ready for Peps' arrival.

Several days later, in the midst of luncheon, Primitivo came running in to say that a plane had circled the airstrip. As I ran down the steps and out into the patio, I saw scores of people running and shouting in the direction of our new airport. Just as I rounded the corner I saw Peps' little yellow Piper Cub approaching the far end of the strip, flying very low. I clutched my two little boys by each hand, and in front of us ran at least fifty farmhands and workmen who were already approaching the strip.

I was terrified, for Peps' plane, although very low, had passed over almost half of the field without having touched the ground, and since the strip was dangerously short, I realized that he might easily crash on the very brief area which remained. Not only that, but I had left two or three trees in a far corner because their beautiful shapes enhanced the view from my bedroom window, and it had seemed to me that a slight curve in the airstrip should not make much difference if it were well marked. Also, the second half of our airport sloped downwards and had been impossible to make as smooth as the first part, which Peps had already left untouched.

I ran towards the field, my legs becoming weak with fear. In one moment I could picture Peps and his plane crashed in a million pieces right there before my eyes, all because of my failure to carry out his instructions to the letter.

By this time the wheels had touched down at the very end of the strip. The disastrous moment had arrived. But miraculously, in a distance of fifty yards the plane managed to stop just at the beginning of a deep rut and a heap of boulders.

By the time the children and I arrived at the plane, Peps was jumping out, much more calm than I. With him had come an American pilot who admitted that as they touched down he had said what he thought were his last prayers.

You can picture the wonder and amazement of all the inhabitants. Not one of them had ever seen an airplane before except flying high in the air. We had to form a human rope around the plane, made up of our most trusty and self-controlled farmhands, in order to keep the plane from being destroyed by the curiosity of these onlookers.

'I only have time for lunch,' said Peps, as he handed me several packages and letters from my house in Madrid. While we were lunching, he explained to me several prime errors in the construction of the airport.

'First of all,' he said, 'the whitewashed stones which I ordered were completely invisible from the air since they had been placed on edge, rather than flat.'

Of course, from the ground these made my strip very conspicuous, but from the air one little whitewashed point of stone now and then meant nothing.

'And,' Peps advised me, 'you must give some sort of lessons in airport precautions. The reason I avoided the first half of the airstrip was because two men on horseback who were casually riding by, and all the workmen immediately swarmed over the field, rather than keeping on the borders, and this created another hazard! If I had not landed when I did, it would have been impossible for me to land at all on any part of the strip.'

After lunch I opened my airmail packages which were brightly wrapped in white paper with long red ribbons, since Peps had thought it possible he might not be able to land and would have to drop them to me.

We walked back to the plane and by now the field was black with people. The entire town of Santa Marta was congregated on our strip and the road to the town was still crowded with villagers arriving from everywhere. It is amazing how in the country, without the aid of telephones and cars, people manage to hear so quickly of any news or exciting event. With great difficulty we cleared the field so that Peps could take off.

The next three days were unbearable because at least three hundred people decided that since the Pascualete airstrip was now officially open, there would be planes arriving daily, and there was no way to convince them that nothing was going to happen and that they should go home.

Our airstrip did much to stimulate my air-mindedness. Shortly after, I had an opportunity to make a trip to the *finca* in the small private plane of an Italian friend of ours. We squeezed ourselves into the little machine one Saturday at Madrid airport and proceeded to taxi out to the runway. I had flown several times with Peps and had the greatest confidence in small planes, but I noticed that this one seemed to give many uncertain jolts even while still on the ground. It occurred to me that possibly Gianni had not exactly found the runway, but as the plane started to lift off the ground, I noticed the same alarming bumps. However, he seemed very busy with the controls, and despite the uncertainty of our beginning, we soon found ourselves at about three hundred feet.

Just as I was about to relax, the most abrupt sideways movement began. It was rather like being in a small boat on a rough sea.

Added to this, sinister bursts of noise, every now and then punctuated by ominous silences, were coming from our only engine. Fortunately we were well strapped into the little plastic-covered cockpit and our great sideways dips had not caused us any harm.

But all of a sudden there was one lasting blast of the engine which ended in a complete silence. I now realized that we were in grave danger, and I remember feeling desperately sorry for my Italian friend who I knew must be enduring not only the normal bad moment of thinking he was going to crash, but added to that the distress of having put me in this danger with him.

The world seemed far below me, but I suddenly recognized a much more imminent danger straight in front of my eyes—a large flat high-tension cable directly in the path of our plane, which was losing altitude every moment. Suddenly Gianni did something which caused the plane to turn and fall sharply to the right. I knew this was the end. At one moment I saw a mass of green rushing up at me, and at the next it was in front of me again. I realized that we were in a wheatfield and I was wondering why we had not crashed yet, when there was a tremendous noise and I tasted the grittiness of earth in my mouth. Great jolts and bounces followed, and suddenly nothing. No green, no sun, no sky, and a great silence. 'How easy it is to be dead,' I thought, and in the same instant I realized that I was very much alive—so much alive that for the first time in the last five minutes I was filled with real terror, when I heard Gianni's voice saying, 'We must get out of here immediately!'

'Yes,' I thought, 'in the movies after one crashes the plane usually burns.'

I managed to undo my safety belt and at the same time I lifted my right hand to undo the clip which permitted the plastic cover of our cockpit to slide backwards. It would not move. By this time Gianni was already trying to pull back his side, and it also would not slide. Again Gianni's voice, 'Push with all your might!' and the two of us at the same time grasped the plastic top and pushed back. Still it would not give. Once again we gathered up our energy. I could tell by Gianni's voice that we were in desperate danger. Somehow this last time we managed to open just enough to permit us to climb out and I heard Gianni say, 'Run as fast as you can!'

I ran. I did not have time to see what had happened to the plane. I ran and ran. Finally I noticed that Gianni, who was running alongside of me, had stopped and turned round. I did the same.

About a hundred yards behind us was a heap of kindling wood. The plane had split at about six inches from the back of our two seats and that part could be seen in another direction about a hundred yards away. The two wings were crumpled into small bits and scattered about the field. My suitcase, which had been just behind my back, was unrecognizable and bits of my clothes were strewn all over the area. As we looked at this sight I felt happy as never before in my life. We grabbed each other and jumped up and down with glee like small children.

Now I could see cars approaching us, driving across country. I recognized my own jeep heedlessly crossing the entire airstrip in order to reach us in the shortest possible time.

In about ten minutes the cars and people began to arrive. Some workmen from a near-by field started to tear at my clothes in order, I discovered, to get pieces for good luck. Others were screaming 'Miracle!' and everybody seemed to be in a frenzy of excitement. I saw Pepe, our driver, appear, green in the face, and when he reached me he put his head on my shoulder and began to cry like a baby.

We were feasted and our rebirth was lavishly celebrated that day in the airport, but it has killed all my desires to travel to Pascualete by plane.

19

Shooting at Pascualete

OVER THE YEARS, our trips to Pascualete have been as regular as the calendar and there are certain times when we are sure to be in residence—week-ends in the autumn and winter for partridge shooting, at Christmas and during Holy Week, and again in the summer for another type of shooting.

Shooting has always been the great passion of my husband and his family, and when I first married I was faced with spending six months a year without a husband or learning how to participate in this difficult sport. I was not enthusiastic at first, but it did not take long for me to become an equally fanatic devotee.

When I heard the first clucking partridge at Pascualete and then saw a mass of fluttering wings arise from a grove of retama bushes and whir off in formation planing gracefully close to the ground, I knew Luis would be spending a lot more time at Pascualete than his late ancestors had done.

And I was not wrong. Luis' first visits to the *finca* were encouraged by the shooting it offered, and once the house was renovated, we began giving organized shoots.

Our most plentiful game is partridge—the red-legged variety —which is a bit smaller than the American or British bird.

'There are many properties where twelve good guns can down as many as two thousand partridge in one day,' I used to hear Spanish shots say, and attributed this to the hunter's natural braggadocio. Like most foreigners in Spain, I found it hard to believe that the Estremanian and Castillian countryside, so sun-baked and dry in summer, can in the autumn yield black clouds of partridges flying in a never-ending stream overhead.

Although I had never shot in America, I had some vague idea that it meant going out with a dog and walking in the fields hoping to flush a covey of birds. But of course, in Spain, as in most of Europe, shooting is completely different.

In Spain, it is the beater who flushes the birds, while one sits behind a butt made of bows of live oak in the company of a gentleman known as a *secretario*. Contrary to what one might think, his main job is not to type or take shorthand, but in moments of crisis his fingers move just as fast. He holds the dog during the shooting, and dispenses free advice and local lore. But most important of all is his role in the great struggle of retrieving.

A day's partridge shoot in Spain is usually divided into five beats, with ten or twelve butts on each beat. About thirty beaters drive the game towards the guns, and these fast small birds offer great sport even for the most expert marksmen. Although foreign guns are always overwhelmed by the abundance of partridge, they are usually pretty dismayed at the end of the day to see how little they have to show for their efforts.

This is no reflection on their shooting ability but rather because of a certain peculiarity in Spanish shooting customs. You see, it is customary for each gun to be accompanied, not only by a *secretario*, but also by a loader for his two shotguns and another man to keep his eye on the falling birds.

The moment the beaters appear in front of the butts each gun sends his two or three men and his dogs swarming out into the field at full speed to recover, apart from his own, as many as possible of his neighbour's birds. I have often watched with amusement the face of a shooting neighbour newly arrived in Spain as he wanders around sadly picking up what the Spaniards on either side have left him. He may have downed eighteen or twenty birds, but if the newcomer goes back to his butt with three birds he is lucky.

Actually, Spaniards are excellent shots, but I am not convinced this is due to any inherent facility so much as the fact that most Spanish shots carry a gun from the age of eight on. What's more, they shoot an average of ten times more cartridges than any foreign gun can during the hunting season, for in Spain it stretches from the middle of September until after the first week in

February. But after participating in many shoots, I have finally decided that Spaniards enjoy retrieving as much as shooting.

'It really is a most unattractive habit,' they will say to you, but show no signs of giving it up. And I must admit that even I do not like to look a fool by allowing others to pick up my birds, so in self-defence I have become just as adept as any Spaniard in grabbing my neighbour's birds.

It is bad form to ask anyone how many birds he has downed the moment the beat is over, because although he may add five or six on principle, he is apt to come back with still more after his foray. At the end of each drive the birds are picked up and dropped in two large saddle bags carried by a donkey and the number retrieved by each gun is carefully marked down in a game book. Each Spanish marksman keeps a careful record of the number of birds he has retrieved during each season. And of course, it may come as no surprise to the reader that some of the most famous shots in Spain are those who are also best at the game of retrieving.

Shooting in other countries seems very tame after Spain. I will never forget a pheasant shoot we attended in France. Two other Spaniards were invited to this glamorous and gentlemanly shoot, where the beaters wore white jackets and were transported to the shoot in trucks. After the first drive, the three Spaniards, with their conditioned reflexes, tore into the field at top speed. But a voice called to them:

'No, you do not have to retrieve your own birds here—the beaters will do that for you.'

Disappointed, the Spaniards waited patiently for someone to inquire of them how many birds each had downed. But the subject never came up and when the beaters retrieved the birds, they were put in a heap, counted and marked on the game card, with no way whatever of telling who had killed what number.

In Spain, the terrain is very rough compared with the pheasant country of France. We usually shoot on hilly, rough ground, often spotted with small live oak trees, quite a contrast to the smooth green lawns around French shooting posts.

A scene during the shoot. The Countess is sitting on a shooting stick with her back to the camera. The Count, half turned toward the camera, is gesticulating with his hand.

After the shoot.
The Countess
trying
to catch
a lamb

Shooting at Pascualete

Since throughout Spain the winter sun shines brightly, we usually eat outdoors on these shoots. After the third drive we stop for lunch. This is more often a large *paella*, a rice dish which in the country is cooked in a two-handled iron skillet, about three feet in diameter. To the rice is added sweet red peppers, saffron, olive oil, chicken or partridge, or often different kinds of sea-food, such as shrimp, crayfish, mussels and clams, with green peas and tomatoes. The secret of its success, however, is the texture of the rice and Spaniards are artists preparing a rice in which each kernel is separate from the other and yet soft.

Great fresh white cheeses, plenty of country bread and lashings of red wine, complete this typical hunters' fare and the shoot is continued until dusk.

During our shooting week-ends we often have many attractive women guests, very smart in their embroidered leather caps and short shooting jackets. I never observed any sort of reaction from the country people, and naturally I assumed this was because of their respect and sense of decorum. Imagine my surprise when one day walking over some particularly rough terrain, Primitivo said to me:

'What good legs that Señora has!'

A bit shocked, I looked ahead at the legs moving in front of me and wondered how Primitivo could have guessed they were particularly decorative as they were well encased in long leather boots and covered far below the knees with classic leather chaps. Seeing my questioning look, Primitivo added:

'Señora Condesa, I mean that the Señora ahead walks better than any man.'

I then realized that her 'good' legs had nothing to do with their proportions, but that his admiration stemmed only from their usefulness.

'*Sí*, Señora Condesa,' Primitivo informed me. 'Many country people are never good walkers, even though they spend their life on foot. To be known as a good walker is a very great compliment.'

*   *   *

Life Today at Pascualete

During the hottest and driest period in Estremadura—mid-August to mid-September—a fascinating phenomenon takes place which provides us with the best shooting of the year—the passing of the turtle-doves. This is the time when the '*tortolas*' gather in great bands to prepare for their yearly migration to Africa. During this period they fly out in droves to the nearest fields to eat grain. Every morning at about six-thirty, just after the sun rises, there is one hour when the birds fly in dark grey clouds from their tree homes to the nearest stubble field to glean the grains of wheat. Then they fly back to their woods. The same procedure takes place about four-thirty in the afternoon, at which time the passing usually lasts longer, perhaps two hours going out and two hours coming back. Each year the '*tortolas*' choose a regular passage to their feeding grounds, and if one places a butt in this passage, well-concealed so that the birds will not see the guns and fly too high, one can have constant shooting during the hours of the passing.

We advise our friends to bring at least one thousand cartridges per day and to take it very calmly and not try to shoot constantly during the first hour. However, newcomers never believe that there is that much shooting available. They always arrive short of cartridges and ruin their shoulders in the first day of shooting. Sometimes even the best guns of Spain are obliged to give up after two days.

Partridge and turtle-doves are by no means our only sport at Pascualete. There are also bands of bustards, relatives of the wild turkey of America—which often weigh twenty-five to thirty pounds and have great white wings and a bewhiskered beak. The white meat of the legs makes delicious eating and the excitement of the chase is worth any effort.

The shepherds know just where these giant birds spend their day and we always consult them before leaving for a day's bustard shooting. We drive in a car or a jeep, with our shotguns cocked, each ready to jump out at a moment's warning, while Primitivo and his little son José go on ahead on horseback. These birds settle principally in treeless areas because they have

such an enormous wing-spread that they have difficulty in taking off if they do not have plenty of space.

Approaching the band, which can consist of five, thirty or even a hundred birds, the two horsemen make a wide circle at an ample distance from the birds and slowly come up behind them. We continue in the car at a slow even pace until we are about two hundred yards from the quarry, at which moment Luis gives the order to jump. Everyone jumps from the moving car, which keeps going at the same pace (if the car stops, the birds will take warning and fly away), and we fall as flat as possible and take cover behind any tall grass or rocks which will shield us from the sight of the birds. We wait breathlessly, not daring to lift our heads from the ground until the flock, aroused by the approach of the horsemen, rises slowly and takes to the air. This is the moment to shoot. IF one is lucky and IF the location has been well chosen and IF the horsemen have driven the birds in the right direction, they usually take to the air just over our heads and it is quite easy to get a shot at them. However, bustards are so heavy and strong one has to get a very direct shot to down them.

Luis' Uncle Eduardo, Conde de Yebes, probably Spain's greatest authority on bird and game shooting, prefers to do his bustard shooting with a rifle. This is very difficult as it is almost impossible to get close enough to these birds on the ground to enable one to take aim and shoot.

One day with Eduardo we sighted two enormous birds about two hundred yards from the path of our jeep. With a minimum of noise we stopped and waited while Eduardo cautiously took his unprepared rifle out of its case, mounted, loaded and primed it against the fender of the jeep. He took aim and pressed the trigger and every moment I expected to see the giant bird take to the air, since we were in plain sight of each other. But I marvelled at Eduardo's coolness and careful preparations, and he later confessed to me that his hands were trembling with excitement despite his many years of shooting. We counted out two hundred and eighty paces to the spot where the great bird lay dead.

Life Today at Pascualete

Luis likes to have stuffed examples of each of our best Pascualete birds and as Eduardo's bustard was an especially large one, we sent it off to a farmer Primitivo had conveniently found who practised taxidermy as a hobby. When our order was returned, the bustard had an electric light bulb hanging from his bewhiskered beak and, protruding from under his tail feathers was a long wire ending in a plug. Evidently, this imaginative artist wanted to make our bustard not only beautiful but practical as well by turning it into a lamp.

The taxidermist had also sent along some pieces of his own, which he hoped we might be interested in acquiring. Among them was a small cinnamon-coloured Pomeranian dog, clutching in his half-open mouth a lady's pocket book. After that we were careful when ordering any pieces to stipulate that no embellishments be employed.

20

Our first Christmas at Pascualete

NOW CHRISTMAS at the *finca* is a matter of routine, but I will never forget the first time I attempted to bring an old-fashioned American Christmas to the inhabitants of Pascualete.

In Spain, the festive celebrations for the birth of Christ take place on January 6, the Day of the Three Kings. This is the day when the Kings come laden with gifts for Spanish children, so of course, most of them have never heard of Santa Claus and December 25 is strictly a religious holiday.

But that year I decided to have an authentic American Christmas, beginning with the tree. This was no easy matter, for Christmas trees are not a Spanish custom and are practically non-existent in Estremadura. And so, I ploughed through mud up to my knees in every Madrid nursery, looking for a tree suitable for our Pascualete Christmas. Four days before Christmas, with the six-foot evergreen tied on top of our jeep we arrived at the *finca* in a downpour which had not let up for two weeks.

In a second jeep I had packed toys and Christmas packages for the shepherds' families and for the people of Santa Marta. I brought also records of Christmas carols and holly, ribbon, multi-coloured balloons and everything else I could think of. The turkeys had been fattening for weeks, according to my instructions to Primitivo.

Indeed, everything was beautifully organized, I thought, and I was looking forward to my fourteen adult guests and my six little guests. But I arrived to find that some of our more recently renovated rooms were barely completed. Two bathrooms were unfinished and furniture, curtains and rugs were piled in disorderly heaps waiting to be placed.

Life Today at Pascualete

As the rain continued it looked less and less like an old-fashioned Christmas and I felt progressively more pessimistic about having picked that December to bring Santa Claus to Pascualete. But there was no time to lose and despite the pouring rain we scrambled over the old arch to string up our coloured lights, and in the centre of the big downstairs hall we set up the tree. And Luis and I became plumbers, painters, and carpenters as we hurriedly arranged the unfinished guest rooms.

The morning of the 23rd I gave strict orders that when the guests began to arrive, not one child, cat, dog or workman was to poke his nose into the patio. But this was a futile exercise, for in every case the newcomer was greeted with a patio swarming with ragged children, barking dogs, and curious cats. By the time the car had come to a stop the Santa Marta workmen who were doing last-minute jobs had left their toils to gape too. And often as not, a few stray turkeys and ducks wandered in, or else the guests' arrival coincided with the cattle returning to their stalls. Poor Primitivo, so grand in his treasured uniform, was hidden by the mob.

Among our Christmas guests was a dear Egyptian friend, Marie de Nametalla, who had agreed delightedly to come, even though I warned her of the hardships.

'Oh, my dear Aline, eet eez not ze first time I come to ze country,' she remonstrated. 'I vizeet many French châteaux. I love ze country and ze wonderfool air.'

I am glad I did not see her face when, accustomed to the impressive homes of her French friends, she first entered the cowpath leading to our farm.

'I nevair sought zat ze country could be so country as zeez,' she remarked to the others in the car with her. (They later told me this.)

When they reached one of our ramshackle white gates she brightened up and exclaimed:

'Ah, zeez eez improving! Zeez must be ze entrance to ze park,' remembering the classic well-kept parks of French châteaux.

Imagine her chagrin as the car bounced over the rutty roads, and by the time she had passed under what I considered our very impressive arch she was already asking the driver if there was a night train to Madrid.

Marie descended from the car wearing some dainty flat gold sandals which she had thought appropriate for walking in the country. She watched, horrified, as great globs of mud oozed over her bright sandals, but somehow she summoned up a very weak 'hello' for Luis and me.

I had been worrying about which room was most suitable for this urban guest and made the mistake of putting her in the room I considered the most picturesque. A couple of hours later one of the maids rushed to me in great distress.

'Señora Condesa, the fireplace in the bedroom of Excelentissima Señora de Nametalla is smoking. And I wish to warn the Señora Condesa that if all the guests insist on three *braseros* apiece, we had better send the jeep immediately to Trujillo to purchase another three dozen.'

I rushed down to find my friend lounging Cleopatra-style on her built-in fifteenth-century wall bed. She was choking from the smoke of the overheated room. I put the fire out in the chimney and opened the windows and doors which led out on to a very wet terrace.

'Ooooh, Aline, please shut ze window. Ze smoke is better zan ze cold. You do not understand that I am a Mediterranean and we need heat. You are from a cold country, you cannot understand zat I will die if you leave ze door open one minute longer.'

I smothered her complaints in a big fur blanket which I threw over everything, including her head, until the room was free of smoke. Then I tried heating the room again with *braseros*. But by this time I realized that the recently finished plaster was exuding quantities of dampness which ran in little rivulets down the whitewashed walls.

'I do not understand how ze rain can penetrate into a strong house like zeez,' my Egyptian friend kept exclaiming. And of course, I did not enlighten her by telling her that none of the walls in her wing had had sufficient time to dry out, and the more she stoked up, the damper it got.

Miraculously, the morning of the 24th dawned bright and sunny, which blotted out the last three days of horror. Every now and then a car filled with Christmas gifts arrived in the patio and our big tree was soon heaped on every side with beautiful coloured packages. The little Pascualete children, now well schooled in the legend of Santa Claus, were constantly peering through the big glass doors to see the transformation that was taking place.

We decided to go to Santa Marta for Midnight Mass and since the roads were impassable except by jeep, we had to squeeze all fourteen of us into two jeeps. It was a hazardous trip, punctuated by shrieks of terror from Marie, but we finally reached the little church to find the whole town awaiting our arrival.

As there was no electricity, there was no light except for the dull glimmer of candles which came from the church door. Don Alonso led us solemnly to the altar where chairs had been arranged on either side. As the Mass began, the children of Santa Marta started to sing. There were no musical instruments to aid them, but this made their little erratic voices all the more touching.

The following morning we were awakened at seven o'clock by the children, impatient to see the tree and toys. We dragged ourselves downstairs and opened the big doors. Of course, our children were beside themselves, but that was nothing compared to the expressions of awe on the faces of Pascualete's little children. Then, somehow, the rules of the game were forgotten and they seemed to think the point was to grab as many toys as their little hands could hold. As a result, everyone ended up with someone else's present, but it did not seen to make any difference.

Christmas night I happened to go into my *guardesa's* house where in front of the fireplace, squatting on the floor were Maria, her sister, their children and both their husbands, with tears streaming down their faces as they hand-peeled hundreds of onions.

Our first Christmas at Pascualete

'What on earth are you doing?' I asked as the stench of onions forced me to go back out into the fresh cool air.

Primitivo followed me explaining, 'The day after Christmas is when we observe the important ceremony of the *matanza*, or the killing and dressing of a pig. We are preparing for tomorrow's ritual. Perhaps the Señora Condesa would like to watch, because the *matanza* in Estremadura is the best in all of Spain.'

I was delighted that finally I was going to see how these people make their delicious sausages and Spanish cured hams—the famous *jamon serrano*.

The next morning I was awakened with a message that the pig-killing specialist from La Cumbre was ill and could not officiate at the *matanza*, but that an amateur from Santa Marta had offered his services.

The fattened pigs had been kept in a separate enclosure for two weeks and had been feasting off the greatest delicacies. They were so huge they could hardly walk, but this morning they were dragged squealing from their last home to an open area where enormous kettles and cauldrons were suspended over a fire. The pigs seemed to know what was going to happen because they put up a great resistance at every attempt to approach them.

Meanwhile the brave young amateur from Santa Marta made a great show with his sharpening of knives and various other implements which were to be used. This *matachin*, or killer, prepared for his great moment by ordering four men to grasp the pig and to tie its hind legs together. Everything seemed to be going on schedule as our hero approached the beast from the back to make the dramatic killing. The idea was to grab the animal just under the chin and, with the edge of the knife, gently stroke its fat neck in order to find the exact spot where the jugular vein was located. He had rubbed the neck up and down several times, but just as he was about to plunge the blade into the centre of the vein, the beast gave a great lurch which threw the knife out of the *matachin*'s hand.

In a quick gesture to recover the knife, in mid-air, his care to keep his left hand properly closed on the pig's snout was relaxed, and in one instant we all saw with horror that the pig's enormous tusks had pierced the *matachin*'s hand, which was now securely gripped in his ugly mouth. Everyone began to scream at once, except the pig, and no effort could make him loose his grip.

A clever farm-hand jabbed the pig's rear with a hot iron which he grabbed from the near-by fire, obliging the beast to open his mouth in a cry. At this very moment the man stuck a large stone in the beast's mouth, which enabled him to keep the mouth open long enough to remove the man's hand.

We immediately sent the defeated *matachin* to Caceres in the car and we spent the rest of the day wondering if he was going to lose his hand. However, country people seem to be well accustomed to accidents of this sort, and they continued their killing with the aid of another amateur who bravely volunteered his services.

Once the two fat pigs were dead, freshly scrubbed buckets were placed under their necks to catch the enormous amount of blood which began to drain. Then all the hairs were carefully singed off the animals' ugly bodies, and the women began with the greatest care to shave every last remnant of hair that might remain on the skin. After that they were scrubbed until they were white.

Only then was the butchery begun. Each ham was very carefully cut off, each organ of the animal was removed and washed in deep buckets of water and laid aside. Now the women bent over their enormous cauldrons preparing the mixture for the sausages and blood puddings.

Meanwhile the onlookers began to drink from large leather wine bags and to dance to simple country tunes. This drama, which had begun at ten-thirty in the morning, was still in full swing at six-thirty in the evening, when Pepe returned to inform us that the *matachin* would not lose his hand.

Holy Week in Trujillo

IN EARLY SPRING Holy Week comes to Spain and a great hush falls over the entire country. All frivolity ceases; even restaurants and stores are closed, and during this week every large city and small village has its religious processions of Saints and Virgins as Spaniards relive the passion, sufferings and death of Christ.

The processions in large cities such as Seville are famous throughout the world; however, in small villages like Trujillo, the medieval atmosphere is apt to be much more authentic, for tourists and sightseers rarely intrude upon the townspeople's sincere and natural expression of their faith.

In these processions—which usually take place Holy Thursday and Good Friday—the Patron Saints or particular Virgins are paraded through the village, accompanied by many of the townspeople, specially costumed and even masked. This procession may last two or three hours and then that particular Saint or Virgin is returned to the church where it normally rests from one year to the next. Each village has its own traditions and costumes for this occasion, some dating back to Roman times. For example, in Toledo the townsmen dress as Roman warriors, complete with breastplates, shields and short skirts. Some are dressed as soldiers and some as centurions with plumed helmets, which gives one an idea of how the Roman army of occupation might have looked. In Trujillo, they usually wear the long flowing robe and pointed hood more often associated with Holy Week processions.

One year, just before we were to leave for our annual Holy Week excursion to Pascualete, I picked up the telephone in Madrid and a voice said:

Life Today at Pascualete

'This is Sister Catherine.'

She explained that a nun who had taught me during my college days had suggested she telephone me on arriving in Madrid. The voice added that she was visiting Spain for the purpose of seeing the Holy Week celebrations, and at the same time to study sixteenth-century architecture.

'Oh, dear!' I thought. 'What shall I do with a nun?' The only solution was to ask her to lunch, which I confess I hoped she would refuse.

'Why, I would be delighted,' Sister Catherine quickly answered. 'But of course, I must bring along the two sisters who are my companions on this trip.'

My three guests arrived five minutes early and when I rushed downstairs, I found each sitting with a Martini in her hand. I wanted to shoot the butler. How could he serve Martinis to nuns! Those poor innocents obviously had no idea what they were drinking. But as soon as we introduced ourselves, Sister Catherine said:

'My, I do love Martinis, and these certainly are good ones!'

After lunch, I happened to complain of a hoarseness which had bothered me for months. Sister Catherine, who among other things was a singing teacher, said she could teach me how to cure this, whereupon, she threw herself to the floor.

'You must lie down,' she said, 'in order to be in a proper breathing position and to relax the abdominal muscles.'

The two others decided to profit from this exercise as well. Just as we lifted our legs in the air, bending them at the knee, the butler appeared with the coffee. I expected the worst. He would drop the tray, spill the coffee, break the cups. But no. Being Spanish and unpredictable, he continued across the room, placed the tray as always on the table and never changed his expression.

Later, Sister Catherine confided: 'You know, we are very tired of visiting museums, palaces and historical monuments. Do you think it would be possible for us to see something different? We would be so disappointed to leave Spain without seeing some of that wonderful gipsy dancing and singing.'

Holy Week in Trujillo

I wondered if the good sisters really knew how wild flamenco could be, but I said I would arrange a flamenco party for them.

I invited Pastora Imperio, the seventy-year-old queen of Spanish gipsies and about ten dancers, singers, and guitarists, all of whom arrived in their gayest costumes about six in the afternoon. When they saw the three elderly nuns, they suddenly forgot how to dance or sing and the first two numbers were a complete failure. But gradually they lost their shyness and my little nuns were delighted with the exhilarating music.

Since my new friends were anxious to witness the most authentic Holy Week processions and since, by this time, I was willing to go to Mars in their delightful company, I offered to take them to Estremadura.

So it was that I arrived in the plaza in Trujillo and startled Pillete by getting out of the car accompanied by three black-habited companions. I explained that I had brought them to see the processions and to do some sight-seeing.

'It is an honour for our city,' said Pillete, who loved to make pompous speeches at the drop of a hat. 'I hope you will find our fair city worthy of such distinguished attention. Unfortunately, the nuns of Trujillo are all cloistered, but I Pillete, will be happy to offer my services as guide.'

It was unusually cold for March, and as Pillete escorted us across the plaza I suggested we sneak into his bar by the back door to decide upon our procedure in warmth and comfort.

Pillete, despite his thick middle, bowed repeatedly as the nuns passed before him through a bad-smelling, dark corridor into a little kitchen where an untidy girl was washing dishes at a sink in one corner and Candida and an old woman were seated at a *mesa-camilla*.

Candida jumped up when she saw the unusual group entering her door, but with great self-control managed to conceal her surprise. Pillete's old mother, bent and almost sightless, tried to bob up from the table to make room for the illustrious guests.

Soon we were all seated snug and warm round the table. In no time four cups of *café con leche* which Candida placed before us were sending up white spirals of steam through the cold air of the room. This little alcove had been constructed in what must have been a great high-ceilinged room in the old palace in which the bar was located, and the walls had been made with windows of glass to permit Candida a surveillance of the goings-on in the bar. We could just see a corner of the long white marble counter where one of Pillete's sons was serving drinks. My nuns seemed enchanted with their environment and in their meagre Spanish tried to converse with Candida.

Although now comfortably warm, foresighted Sister Catherine inquired where we could get her some woollen socks for our sightseeing tour. I then remembered that in my overnight bag in the car were a pair of luminous shocking pink anklets.

'I will be delighted to have you borrow mine,' I told her, 'but I warn you they will not go very well with your habit.'

In view of the temperature outside, she waved aside that little detail, and Pillete went scuffling out to the car to bring my bag.

The kitchen was so small that we were frequently sprinkled by the energetic dish-washer, and Candida's big, brown-eyed child sat on Sister Ann's lap where she goggled fascinated when Sister Catherine calmly removed her black shoes and began to put on the bright pink socks. Pillete bolted out of the room, embarrassed at the very thought of seeing a nun's bare stockinged foot. I ran after him to remind him to telephone to the Mothers Superior of the convents we were to visit.

I rather imagined that my nuns had seen quite a few convents in their lives, but it just happens that in Trujillo the most ancient and beautiful buildings belong to religious orders. My American nuns got along wonderfully with their Spanish sisters who tried hard not to show their surprise at the glaring pink additions to Sister Catherine's habit.

We went from one palace to another with plump Pillete running ahead to warn of our arrival. Incredulous, Pillete watched every gesture of the American sisters. I could see that his natural Spanish reverence for a nun was mixed with his growing admiration for the warmth and courage of our American visitors. He was at their beck and call and on the eve of Good Friday he begged Sister Catherine for the honour of having them view the next evening's *pasos* from his house.

Therefore, the night of Good Friday we gathered on the balcony of Pillete's lovely old house facing the great doors of the church of San Francisco to watch the Procession of Silence—so called because on this night of Christ's death the procession takes place in complete silence.

Below us hundreds of black-robed figures were forming two lines on either side of the church entrance. They wore high pointed black hoods which completely masked their faces except for two slits for the eyes, and each of these 'penitents' carried a long candle. The spectators were subdued, but there was an air of expectancy which made one realize that something important was about to happen.

With the roll of the drums there appeared in the doorway the enormous float bearing the figure of the Virgin. Reigning over a platform ablaze with hundreds of tiny candles whose white flames danced and swayed in a constant mysterious movement, the Virgin was dressed in ancient robes of silk and lace and wore a crown encrusted with sparkling gems. Many of the towns-people on whose shoulders the float was carried went barefoot as a penance. At first, I used to feel terribly sorry for those men who carried the heavy float, but later I learned that they vie with each other for the honour and theirs is the most coveted post of the procession.

The instant the procession began there was silence throughout the city, except for the slow, mournful beat of the drums. And only the hundreds of small candles they carried outlined their progression through the narrow, tortuous streets.

Suddenly, from a darkened corner of the crowded street, we heard an eerie, plaintive song. It was a *saeta*, literally an arrow of song, a spontaneous eulogy sung to the Virgin by someone overcome in the dark silent night by adoration and religious ecstasy. This song of passion and pathos, simplicity and fervour, expressed the devotion and faith of each of us who listened, hypnotized.

When the singing began the procession had stopped, and those carrying the Virgin had placed the dias so that She faced the singer until the song was finished. The Virgin acknowledged the singer's tribute with a bow and the procession began to move again. Slowly the two glimmering lines of candles wound their way through the narrow streets until they disappeared into the darkened city.

This ritual, stemming from the days when Christianity first came to Spain, each year is re-enacted in this poignant and dramatic manner.

Trujillo's other major holiday is as gay and abandoned as the Holy Week celebration is ritualistic and solemn.

It amuses me to think that the big popular fiesta of Trujillo commemorates the day that Pascualete's first owner, Fernan Ruiz, opened the gates to let the Christian soldiers into the city and thus defeat the Moors.

This 'Day of Victory,' is celebrated every October 18 and is the occasion of Trujillo's smaller version of the 'running of the bulls' such as takes place in Pamplona.

Every year we are invited by one of Trujillo's merchants to view the excitement from his store balcony which overhangs the narrow street where the bulls run up to the plaza.

The first time we went I wanted to take my two older boys with me, but our English Nanny was very much opposed.

'Madam, it is a crime to take innocent lads to see such a barbarian spectacle. It will twist and warp their little minds just like these cruel Spaniards.'

'Nanny, I will not have you speak that way,' I retorted indignantly. 'Remember, please, that we are Spaniards and so are my little boys. And bullfighting is no more cruel than that famous English sport of chasing the fox. Furthermore, the celebration in Trujillo is not a real bullfight. It's merely a running of the bulls and they don't kill them and no blood is spilled.'

Although thoroughly annoyed with her attitude, I wanted her to come with us. I was sure that in the end she would enjoy it.

When we arrived at our balcony, the entire length of the winding street had been boarded off so the bulls could not escape. Here the town youths ran in front of the bulls all the way up to the plaza.

My children squealed with joy when they first glimpsed the young Trujillans, screaming with panic, as they ran up the narrow street, the bulls in hot pursuit.

'Now children,' Nanny was saying, 'you don't have to look. Look at the pretty flags across the way.'

'But Nanny, we like to look at the bulls, and maybe someone will get hurt,' said my little five-year-old, at which I thought Nanny would have apoplexy.

Actually, my little boy's hope could easily have come true. When that first bull with its enormous horns rounded the corner I had to admit I was frightened. Every now and then one of the running youths fell, but each time miraculously avoided a goring by scrambling up the iron gratings which covered most of the windows along the street. In a few moments the herd of roaring bulls and terrified boys had passed by our balcony.

'*Que peña, Mamá,*' said Alvaro, 'nothing happened.'

This was just the beginning. On arriving at the plaza which had been enclosed with wooden planks to form a bullring, the bulls were penned in log enclosures until the *corrida* began. Today there were no bullfighters, this honour having been reserved for the town's young men who wished to show off their bravery and skill.

As each bull was released, an *aficionado* jumped into the ring with an improvised bullfighter's cape. The bulls, of course, were not the average five-year-olds encountered in the Madrid bull-ring, but they looked strong enough to do a great deal of damage. The movements of these would-be bullfighters were so amateurish that I was sure they would be gored to pieces. But Nanny could only say, 'Humph, serves them right. Grown men teasing that poor beast.'

Pillete's five sons darted in and out of the ring constantly during this catch-as-catch-can *corrida*. And each time one went into the fray, Pillete and Candida, astride the wooden benches forming one side of the ring, started gesticulating and shouting to their sons.

I could not hear what they were saying, but I could see Pillete, his face red with anger, screaming at his sons and pointing towards the bar. Obviously he was ordering them to go to work, but this was one day when the boys dared to defy their father.

Now I saw a figure alone in the middle of the ring, ordering the other would-be fighters to retire, almost with the authority of a real matador. Not until the children started clapping their hands and screaming, '*Olé, Pepe! Olé!*' did I recognize our chauffeur.

His first passes were certainly theatrical if not classic. I stood hypnotized with fear as the great pointed horns each time missed Pepe's body by an eighth of an inch. Nanny turned ashen. But the children were ecstatic and so was the crowd, when suddenly that sharp, curved right horn, like a fine needle going through silk, punctured what appeared to be Pepe's left thigh, and he was thrown high in the air and dumped like an old sack of dirt into a corner of the ring.

I grabbed the children so they would see no more and rushed from the balcony. In my misery and confused mental state I was beginning to think perhaps Nanny had a point after all.

'Well,' she said, visibly shaken but with a grim set look on her face. 'I suppose now, Madam, you will understand why this is not recommended for youngsters.'

'Mamá,' Alvaro asked, 'is Nanny upset because we don't have Pepe to drive the car any more?'

I thought it best not to answer. There was no way to get near the ring to find out what had happened, so the children and I walked towards the car. When we arrived, there stood a sheepish Pepe, badly messed up, but miraculously alive and waiting to serve us.

Holy Week in Trujillo

'Pepe, Pepe,' the children screamed. 'We saw you and you were the bravest matador of all. *Muy hombre, eh Mamá?* When I grow up I want to be a matador like Pepe.'

I was not exactly pleased to hear that, and as I rode home I wondered how many Trujillan boys had been hurt in this tempestuous yearly celebration since the day the Arabs were conquered and driven out of the city.

22

Digging up the Giant Warrior

Although I had solved the mystery of Pascualete's past, I did not abandon my interest in the historical characters I met during my investigations, nor did I stop attending my *tertulia*.

One day, when I walked into the *tertulia*, I heard Miguel Canilleros remark, 'We have just received permission to disinter "the body".'

This news seemed to please the members immensely and there was no way of interrupting their boisterousness long enough to discover to whom 'the body' belonged. Everyone seemed to be on such intimate terms with the corpse that I was just about convinced they were referring to the President of the Academy of History who had died the previous week. Finally, seeing my perplexed look, one of my friends enlightened me.

'We are at last going to disinter the body of Diego Garcia de Paredes,' he said, 'the fifteenth-century warrior reputed to be the strongest and most gigantic Spaniard in history.'

I remembered having seen Diego's crypt on the left-hand side near the entrance door to the church of Santa Maria in Trujillo. And on the other side of the door still stands the huge holy water font which at one time he had removed from its pedestal in a far corner. Legend has it that when Diego as a young man was leaving Mass one day with his mother, she exclaimed that she had forgotten to bless herself. Diego insisted that she remain where she was and he would bring the Holy Water to her. He ran into the church, picked up the stone font which today six men cannot lift and placed it on the floor in front of her. It has remained there ever since.

I also remembered another amusing story about Diego's love

affair with a noble lady of Trujillo whom he used to visit late at night. The only entrance to her room was through her bedroom window which was protected by the typical heavy iron grating. In order to preserve her honour and prevent people from knowing exactly which lady was his mistress, Diego broke the bars of all the windows on that street. As proof today people point to a particular narrow street in Trujillo where there are a number of old palaces and where the bars of every window are missing.

Realizing that Diego's name was familiar to me, the Count of Canilleros went on to explain:

'Diego had an illegitimate son who was a great conquistador and founded the city of Trujillo in Venezuela. Now the Venezuelan government has sent representatives to Spain to request permission to open the father's tomb in order to copy for their museum any arms which might have been interred with the body. And the members of the *tertulia* have been invited to take part in the ceremony.'

During the following months we discussed the opening of old tombs in every phase and form. Some were most optimistic about finding Diego lying in state, well preserved with his arms and sixteenth-century dress, but others claimed that not even the dust of his bones would remain.

Diego had gone to Italy to fight against the French and he died in Bologna in 1532. But his legitimate son, who lived in Trujillo, had the body brought to Spain in 1545 and buried there. It was generally supposed that Diego had made the trip from Italy in a heavy lead casket typical of that period. Although the trip might have been rough and jolted him around a bit, a well-made sixteenth-century coffin certainly might have preserved the contents.

After weeks of speculation the disinterring of Diego Garcia de Paredes was set for July 18, some two months hence. A prominent Spanish doctor and a dentist were invited to take part in the ceremony and I opened Pascualete to all the members of the *tertulia* who wished to come.

Late in the afternoon of July 17 we arrived at the plaza of Trujillo. It was hot and very quiet except for the storks on the church steeples clacking their bills with noisy insistence until we looked up to admire their newly-made golden nests, sparkling in the sun and bulging out around the narrow belfry. (Throughout Spain a nest of storks flourishes in every church steeple and superstition has it that to kill a stork brings bad luck.)

While we waited for the others of our group to arrive we sat at a little table in front of the Bar Imperio sipping aperitifs. Finally when we had all gathered, we ordered dinner.

Pillete served us, openly disapproving of our gloomy conversation about corpses. By the time the meal was over he could bear it no longer and he turned to Luis with a hearty guttural laugh and said:

'Ah, Señor Conde, I have not told you about the riot I caused in Madrid at the Teatro Martin. I grabbed the big toe of the dancer as she came out on the runway and they nearly had to close the whole theatre the way people laughed when she screamed at me. She was a hot-tempered wench and damned good-looking too.'

'But Pillete, how did Candida ever let you get away with that?'

His rumbling laugh burst out in full force now, and we were obliged to join in as he confessed that he had managed to have this little escapade away from his wife's ever-vigilant eyes.

The agreeable freshness of the evening—as soon as the sun goes down in Spain it becomes cool—and the bright moonlight playing on the shadows of the arches held us entranced, and it was two o'clock before we felt inclined to take the path to Pascualete.

The following day the dust of our cowpath from Pascualete to Trujillo was so thick that we were obliged to stop every ten minutes for a breath of fresh air, so we arrived late to the plaza. Our small group rushed up the cobble-stoned street to the church of Santa Marta as quickly as the heat of the day would permit. As I arrived at the enormous church doors I could hear from within the ominous sound of a pickaxe striking against stone and I was relieved to know that the crypt had not yet been opened. After passing through the large crowd at the entrance, I pressed against

A bathroom in
Pascualete; the
Countess and
Maria, the
Guardesa

One of the many fireplaces at Pascualete

the old wooden door and felt the refreshing cool air of the church rush against my face.

Once inside the dim church with its beautiful Gothic arched ceilings I could distinguish my friend the Conde de Canilleros surrounded by several Venezuelan dignitaries, standing just in front of the stone tomb where two perspiring shirt-sleeved grave-diggers were hacking away with their iron picks. Miguel Canilleros immediately came towards me and after scolding me for being late, placed me behind the hard-working men so that I would have the best possible view the moment the stone was removed. But in four hundred years this enormous granite block had settled very firmly into place, so I had time to look about me.

There were all the friends I had made since my discovery of Estremadura. Padre Tena was standing to one side holding his little round priest's hat in his hand. I knew he was in a world of his own. No one would be more interested than Father Tena, because Diego Garcia de Paredes was a closer friend of his than anyone present. Only he knew all the little details of the great man's life. He probably even knew the name of the mysterious lady which Diego had been so careful not to disclose.

Most of my *tertulia* friends from Madrid had turned up; my friends the Hornedos were also in the crowd. Even Pillete was standing at a respectful distance and with an appropriate expression of solemnity on his usually jovial round face. The little bootblack was straining his eyes from a far corner; the Mayor of Trujillo stood very pompous and serious near us in the front row, and even the young man I had bought my six pigs from was there too.

I could see the first signs that the stone was giving way and finally the two gravediggers with several mighty heaves managed to throw it backward to the floor at my feet. At first glance, the crypt revealed several odd bones protruding from a mound of dust. There was a general pushing towards the front so that the two gravediggers were nearly shoved into the gaping hole themselves.

Now they decided that two other stones on either side must be removed in order to see the interior properly. This retarded things another ten minutes, but when they were finally removed we all looked into a long dark crypt, full of a fine grey dirt, from which protruded a confused jumble of bones. There were no weapons, no remnants of clothing, not even a skull to indicate which might have been the head or foot of the tomb.

Everyone looked at Miguel Canilleros to determine what was the next move. At that moment Miguel looked as confused as everyone else, but he whispered to me:

'We must find a box in which we can put these bones. They are obviously not the remains of Paredes, who must be in a lead casket underneath. These bones probably belong to descendants of his who were buried here at a later date.'

One of the priests got a large drawer from some refectory cupboard, and this was placed on the floor in front of the open crypt. The gravediggers then began to remove with their bare hands all the bones in the tomb.

Every now and then they were obliged to shovel out on to the floor great mounds of the dirt in which these bones were submerged. Finally, the large grubby hand of one of the gravediggers held up a skull so small that we knew these bones could not belong to our great Diego. Two minutes later the other gravedigger produced another skull, and in the following five minutes four skulls were removed. The mountain of odd bones piling up in the wooden drawer belonged to four people and all of them, according to the doctor, were of a size to indicate persons of a smaller stature than the gigantic Diego.

As the gravediggers continued their task I knelt down in order to peer better into a far corner where the dust and bones had still not been removed. At the same time I saw a glint of metal in a far corner. Curious, I could not resist sticking my head deep into the crypt. Without realizing it, I found my hands delving into the soft powder and was nearly asphyxiated by a strong strange odour —the stagnant air of centuries. I just had time to grab the little piece of metal which proved to be a shoebuckle. By this time we were uncovering bits of old silk and velvet and pieces of shoes and

Digging up the Giant Warrior

I was covered from head to foot with a fine dust and the heavy suffocating scent.

In view of these discouraging revelations, it was decided that Diego's lead casket was probably embedded elsewhere in the church. Miguel Canilleros pointed to the stone slab on the floor directly in front of the crypt and the gravediggers set to work once again to lift this still larger and heavier piece of granite.

We had to back away to allow them room and on looking down I noticed something familiar about its worn *escudo*. I was about to turn and ask Miguel to look again at the *escudo*. Although it was almost unrecognizable it could not be that of Paredes because—I looked more closely—because it was the five roses. They were going to open a Loaisa tomb by mistake! Should I tell Miguel? No, why should I? There would never be another opportunity to view the open crypt of one of the ancient owners of Pascualete. Maybe at last I could find out what one of my ghosts looked like!

I looked up and caught the eye of Father Tena. He knew whose tomb this was. Would he say anything? He stood with his hands clasped before him, waiting calmly and with a very slight smile on his face. He knew also how excited I was.

I stood riveted to the spot, terrified someone else might recognize the *escudo* before the slab had been removed. Slowly, very slowly the great stone lifted out of place and this time there was a general murmur of approval as the dusty lid of an ornate casket appeared in view. Miguel Canilleros' voice stilled the crowd:

'You will have to give more room here. Please back up so the men can work.'

The gravediggers looked very sceptical about lifting the heavy casket from its hole.

'This thing is so tightly wedged in here, Señor Conde, that we would have to remove the slabs on either side in order to get it out.'

'No, no, we cannot do that. We only have permission to open the tomb of Paredes. You will have to see if the lid can be prized open just as it is. Anyhow, that way the remains will not be moved or shaken.'

While some finer tools were being sent for, the onlookers walked about the church again talking in small groups. I kept my place on the edge of the crypt and tried not to show my excitement.

Eventually the lead cover showed signs of giving. Since it would not swing up, it was loosened on all sides and then men lifted it off the box. The surge of the crowd made me grab on to my nearest neighbours in fear of being thrown into the yawning hole, but I quickly caught my balance and looked down. There, grinning up at us, was a shining ivory skull resting on a red damask pillow. The rest was covered by the white robe and green cross of the Order of Alcantara. Two bony hands rested on what looked like an old manuscript on his chest. A light grey film seemed to cover everything; it was as if a grey chiffon cloth separated him from us. There was something incredibly shocking at the way the skull kept grinning, mocking all of us who stood looking down at him in his gruesome bed.

'Somebody should read those papers,' Miguel said. 'We must not disturb the remains but the manuscript must be removed.'

For a moment no one dared to stir. We stood as paralysed. The skulls and bones which had just been removed from the other dirt-laden crypt seemed playthings in comparison with this lone skull laughing up at us.

'Here, Paco!' Miguel called to one of the gravediggers, 'will you remove that paper from the casket? Be careful, now—we do not want to disturb anything.'

The man reached out towards the paper. Very gingerly he tried to slide it loose. As he did so the bony fingers moved, they came loose and rolled sideways and as they rolled they disappeared into dust into the air. The manuscript was now free. Only four fingers remained intact on the white mantle.

Miguel did not even want to touch the paper which the gravedigger stretched up to give him. He leaned close to me and whispered:

Digging up the Giant Warrior

'I cannot bear to touch any of this. Old bones give me the shudders.'

Antonio Rodriguez-Monino and I both grabbed for the manuscript. As we looked down together at the familiar sixteenth century script Antonio began to read. There was a general scramble by those behind to get closer and now the murmur of various voices broke into the awed quiet, but Miguel and I heard only Antonio's low voice:

> *'Como te ves, me ví;*
> *Como me ves, te verás;*
> *Piensalo y no pecarás.'*

(Once did I look as thou who seest me;
As I now am, thou wilt thyself see;
Think on this and thou no sinner wilt be.)

I felt a sudden shiver. I looked up at Miguel and Antonio. They too were shaken. Padre Tena was nodding his head ever so slightly, but otherwise tranquil and unmoved. What had begun as a light-hearted undertaking had turned into a sudden, uncomfortable intimacy with death.

'This cannot be the body of Paredes,' said one of the Venezuelans. 'This man is far from the size of the giant. In fact, he is shorter than average and there are no arms or weapons in this casket either. All the authorities of the period certified that Paredes was interred with his sword.'

'No, obviously this is not Paredes. But the document is definitely sixteenth century, that is obvious from the script,' Antonio answered.

'Let's get that thing covered up again in a hurry,' Miguel said, and he leaned down to order the workers to replace the lid and close the tomb.

'You had better put this back in place,' added Antonio as he handed over the old parchment to Paco, the gravedigger.

'What a strange thing,' he went on, 'that this old quotation should have been interred with this fellow. How did he know his tomb was going to be opened one day? It just goes to prove to you that this idea of preserving one's remains in a lead casket or marble mausoleum is morbid and grotesque. Believe me, I am going to leave instructions that I be buried in a simple pine box in the earth. One that will fall apart quickly so that my dust will lose itself in the earth and so no one can dig me up and play with my remains.'

My frivolous, curious mood had disappeared. I suddenly felt cold. The thick stone walls of the church were far too efficient an insulation against the July heat. I needed some fresh air, sunlight and warmth.

The two gravediggers began to hammer the lid of the mysterious Loaisa tomb into place again. Who was he, this sixteenth century Loaisa who had come out of the past to give me this warning? How had I missed this tomb when I studied so carefully the floor of the church?

Now there was a huddle to decide upon the next move. Some were in favour of taking up the stones on either side of the Paredes tomb, but the Bishop shook his head in disapproval. The Venezuelan group were not to be defeated, however, and suggested removing the bones of the first crypt, which were lying on the floor in the open drawer, to the sacristy for a minute study.

By the time I reached the sacristy, everybody had a bone of some sort in his hands. The doctor was measuring a thighbone which the Venezuelan group had decided was of distinctly larger proportions than the others and could have belonged to Paredes. Miguel Canilleros was of the opinion that none of the bones could have possibly belonged to the great warrior.

I eventually got disentangled from all the old bones and walked hurriedly towards the door. The Loaisas' slab was back in place and only the dark hole of the Paredes crypt was still open awaiting the return of its old bones. I rushed to breathe in the stifling July air outdoors and found the two gravediggers on the church steps, each calmly smoking a cigarette and commenting on the day's work.

Digging up the Giant Warrior

'What has happened is that somebody has opened the Paredes tomb before—that's why all those bones are so mixed up. Now that second tomb has not been touched since the day that old guy was tucked away there. It certainly makes one think—I mean about us all going to look like that one day.'

I leaned on the stone railing waiting for my friends inside, and when they finally joined me we walked together to the plaza where we prepared to enjoy a typically hearty Spanish meal. But I found that everything tasted wrong. With each piece of bread I could see the brown spongy interior of all those ancient bones and even my after dinner cigarette seemed to be permeated with the disagreeable heavy odour.

Musing about the day's macabre adventures I reflected that we may not have discovered the remains of Diego Garcia de Paredes, but by the time I got into the car to go to Pascualete, I had heard and even tasted nothing else for most of the day and indeed I felt much closer than I would have cared to that great Spaniard.

When I returned to the *finca* that night, I drove once more under that familiar arch bearing its proud *escudo*. Maria and Primitivo were awaiting me. They opened the heavy doors and I walked across the rough cobbled floor into the cool, silent house. After all, despite Pascualete's seven hundred years, nothing really had changed.

The same silence pervaded the house, the same smell of burning encina branches. And in the morning I would walk across the rolling fields, perhaps just as Alvaro de Loaisa had done, even as Pascual Ruiz. The people tilling the multi-coloured earth would speak and move in much the same way those others did so many years ago. Pedro the shepherd, Paco the cowherd, Primitivo and Maria—they had always been in Pascualete and they always would be.

Epilogue

IT IS ALMOST TEN YEARS now since that night we discovered Pascualete—dark and isolated, bare and cold, its great stone walls, ancient arches and worn *escudos* inviting us into a strange unknown world.

Today, as I look about me, I find it hard to believe that Pascualete had ever been abandoned, for now this house and its people have become so much a part of our lives.

Now when I try to describe the 'before' of Pascualete's transformation, I find my friends somewhat incredulous. For this reason I like my guests on their first visit to arrive in the evening so that they too will experience something of that feeling of mystery and adventure I felt that first night.

Today, visitors approach the house by eight kilometres of passable country road—no twists and turns, no ruts as before. They drive into an empty patio, where Primitivo, completely at ease in his uniform awaits them. Inside, our guests will find electricity and running water and certain other modern innovations. But despite these concessions to comfort, we have done our best to maintain Pascualete's fifteenth century atmosphere— especially in the dining-room where we dine by the light of candles although we now have a separate kitchen and the meal is no longer cooked in front of us at the huge open fireplace.

Although I see Pascualete as it is, a sprawling, somewhat haphazard but warmly attractive country home—my servants and the people of Santa Marta still insist on calling it a 'palacio'. Invariably, when I arrive from Madrid Maria will report, 'Oh, Don Alonso was here last week with some very important people from Plasencia who wanted to see the *palacio*. Very impressed they were, too.'

A family picture in the carriage. Audrey Hepburn and her husband, Mel Ferrer, are in the foreground

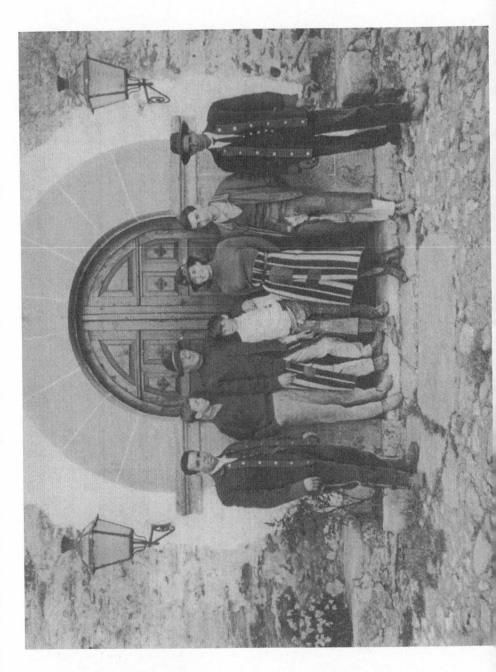

The author and her husband with Luis, Miguel and Alvaro and two guards in front of the main door in the house.

Epilogue

Indeed, Don Alonso takes as much pride in the house as Primitivo and Maria, and it is one of his greatest pleasures to show it off to visitors and act as guide. I shudder when now and then I overhear his exaggerated comments.

'Eighteen fireplaces burn in Pascualete on a winter's day,' I hear him say. 'Five times the Señora Condesa has torn them down and rebuilt them so that not one chimney now smokes. Pascualete is not like those old palaces where one cannot stay for the smoke.'

And on and on he goes, 'Bathrooms, just like in the big cities with all the latest improvements. Hot water at any hour—well, that is at any hour the fireplace in the kitchen and dining-room is burning. And the electricity! Why the motor here is so powerful that all the hundreds of bulbs of the house and even those of the living quarters off the patio are able to work at the same time.'

Don Alonso's explanations of the benefits of electric lights are apt to get lengthy. 'We still do not have electricity in Santa Marta. Here at Pascualete everything is bright and gay at night with the light. In Santa Marta everyone is in bed an hour after sundown. Where there is no light there is no life or happiness,' he says.

The young priest's greatest joy, however, is our chapel, which he considers more his own work. It is almost completely renovated. The walls of the vaulted interior are now a pristine white and everything is in readiness for the celebration of our first mass there.

Naturally, Primitivo and Maria still regard many of my American notions with a mixture of suspicion and condescension. One of my most recent innovations was a refrigerator—a kerosene shelvador we laboriously hauled in by oxen, and which of course, did not work.

'Never mind, Señora Condesa,' Maria consoled me. 'It is a lovely cabinet for storing our eggs in. And really, one could not expect such a machine to make ice.'

Of course, she was perfectly right, because until a battery of experts from Madrid had made several visits to repair it, the

Epilogue

'machine' did not work. So you see, it continues to be quite a struggle to prove that modern civilization occasionally has a few advantages.

The airport never flourished and finally went into disrepair, but we built a makeshift golf course for which the airport served as a perfect fairway. Also, Primitivo solved the problem of maintenance of the grass simply by letting the sheep pasture there.

But the patio! Alas, when I come out to the landing on the steps, I no longer find the bustle and noise of those first years. And I must confess that a neat and orderly patio does not give me half as much pleasure as I thought it would. The animal shelters have been changed so that they can be entered from outside and thus the enchanting nightly procession of the cattle returning to their stalls never takes place within our view. At least, this keeps the animals from doing their 'necessities' just where a guest will have to step on alighting from her car, but now I realize that I like the patio best with all the confusion and even the dirt.

We are no longer absentee landlords for we realized that it was very much to our benefit to farm Pascualete ourselves. Nevertheless, Juan, our former *arrendatario*, and his three brothers often visit us. Juan's son, Andres, has a flourishing bakery in Trujillo and Juan and his brothers are living off their savings in a village about eight kilometres away called Ibahernando. There they each have several acres of rich land and they also have vineyards. Whenever I visit them I am obliged to test their wine, which is so strong and heady that I have difficulty finishing one glass.

But all the others—the shepherds, the cowherds and the farmers who have always worked at Pascualete—are still with us. We have persuaded some of them to move into more modern quarters with running water and bathrooms, but neither they nor I find that these new rooms have as much charm as the old. Most of the children have grown tall, and little José no longer shows any traces of epilepsy and he goes to a boarding school in Caceres where he is an excellent student.

Of course, the people of Santa Marta seem like old friends by now—and Don Alonso has done wonders for his pathetic little village. The young priest, today thirty years old, has obtained the permit for electricity for the town, built a cinema, made a workshop for the jobless which helps them to make money doing straw mats and embroidery and rugs, and has taken advantage of every opportunity to better the life of his parishioners.

In Trujillo, Pillete has prospered. With the profits from his restaurant, bar and ice factory, he has been able to buy a small apartment in Madrid where he spends three months of the winter. But whenever he learns that we are going to Pascualete for any length of time, he will go along too. 'The Señora Condesa is going to be lost without Pillete,' he insists, and of course, he is right. Most of his sons are now married and have supplied him with a host of grandchildren, many of whom look like miniature Pilletes.

Padre Tena is now in his eighties. He continues his rounds to the convents and still pores over his books, although he may walk a bit more slowly up the steps to the archives and he sometimes complains that his eyesight is failing.

Caceres, thanks to my friend the Conde de Canilleros, has become a greater part of my life and my interest in Estremadura has taken me to most of the beautiful old cities of that province many times.

My work in palaeography continues. Now I am not only well versed on the history of Pascualete, but also I am on intimate terms with many other ancient Estremanians. Some of my articles have been published and as a result of my writing about the Conquistadores of Venezuela, I was made a member of the Institute of History of that country.

Federico Hornedo, who first initiated me into the club of Estremanian farmers, is very important in our lives. He is now the administrator of the *finca* and he has taught us how to run it. We often stop by his house in Trujillo—and have lunch with his wife and now six children before going on to Pascualete. And incidentally, the Casa de la Boveda is still a mystery.

Our shooting week-ends are our gayest times. Our friends usually arrive on a Friday night and we start out early Saturday

Epilogue

morning for a day's shooting. At night, when we return to the *finca*, I am invariably questioned about the mysterious names which the guests find on their doors—Pascual Ruiz, Alvaro de Loaisa, and 'The Room of the Four Sisters'. And when I start to explain, Luis shudders and says, 'Oh, no—not that story again!'

Originally I gave each room the name of an important former owner of Pascualete for practical reasons—to avoid confusion in assigning guests to their respective rooms and to help the servants in determining where each piece of luggage went.

But aside from the practical considerations, I have a sentimental reason as well. After these years of historical investigations, I have learned that the name of a room, a house, a hill or even a *finca* often provides one with enough clues to help unravel its history or significance. Names pass down from one generation to another and are not forgotten. And so I hope that these names will continue to mean something to my children's children and to those who come after them, and that one day even Luis and I will not be forgotten and be remembered as a part of the saga of Pascualete.

APPENDICES

THE CONQUISTADORES

The discovery of the New World in 1492 brought great changes to Estremadura, as it did to all the known world at that time. So many famous Estremanians went to the New World at the beginning of the sixteenth century that I am going to mention only a few personal notes about those who came from small villages nearest to our *finca*.

If one has seen the barren land of Estremadura one can understand the hardiness of these men. Likewise one can understand their willingness to face unknown dangers, in their desire to escape the tedious life in Estremadura. In summer the dry sun-baked plains are thick with the accumulated dust of many months without rain. There are few large trees to give shade and often in winter there is a bitter wind or driving rain. Their meagre diet of crude dark brown olive oil and heavy unleavened bread is rarely varied by a piece of meat or an egg.

As a result men were bred who could withstand the hardships of an unconquered tropical continent. Malaria mosquitoes could not get through their leathery skins to the bloodstreams, and they seemed immune to the dysentery which had overtaken the German, English and French would-be conquerors before them. Lack of food supplies during periods lasting sometimes for several months did not kill them, for they were able to eke out a subsistence on any roots or herbs which were to be found.

For example, Francisco Pizarro at the age of forty-five embarked upon the discovery of Peru after spending twenty-three years in different parts of the New World. And because of his rugged Estremanian background he was able to accomplish almost superhuman feats of strength and endurance. He crossed rivers, sometimes carrying soldiers twenty years younger than himself on his shoulders, and he was always at the head of his men in skirmishes with the Indians.

Francisco Pizarro was the illegitimate son of a Trujillan nobleman but was always very close to his five half-brothers. He left Trujillo as a young man, and the only time he returned to Spain, after twenty-five years' absence, he went immediately to his old home where he found that his father had died. But the oldest legitimate son, Hernando, was more than proud to have as a half-brother a man who had been in all the awesome corners of the New World. The curiosity which all Spaniards felt for the New World was such that every poor family and wealthy nobleman dreamed of the possibility of making the trip himself and coming back covered with glory and laden with gold.

When Francisco presented to his friends and his half-brothers his plans for the discovery of far greater wealth than that which had been discovered, they helped him obtain ships and money for his new expedition, and two of the brothers accompanied him on his return.

Pizarro's actual conquest of Peru in 1532 took only eight months, but his preparation was long and tedious. When, halfway between Panama and Peru, the men accompanying him began to complain bitterly about their hardships and lack of food, Pizarro decided to continue only with those who were completely in agreement with the journey, and he drew a line in the sand of the beach and told those men who wished to follow him to step on his side of the line. Those who wanted to return could have one of the boats and enough provisions to make the trip back. Thirteen men stepped over the line, and nine of these men were Trujillans.

After taking the great city of Cuzco from the Incan Emperor, Pizarro made the strategic decision to marry one of the Emperor's two daughters, thereby gaining the backing of the largest and strongest group of Indian natives in that part of the world. He was at this time about fifty years old. Although he never married this Incan Princess within the Catholic church, he lived with her for four years and she gave him a daughter and a son. Later

Pizarro began an alliance with her sister, who had remained unmarried, and who bore him another son.

When he was about fifty-eight years old Pizarro was betrayed by the son of his old friend Almagro and some of his followers and massacred in a hand-to-hand fight. Almagro took over control of the new colony and all Pizarro's followers lost their power and also the favour of Charles V.

Pizarro's three children were cared for by friends and hidden in fear of the dangers of falling into the hands of the new government. During the years when these children were growing up, there continued to be skirmishes with the Indians in Peru, and many months of hardship and hunger. Two sons died and when the daughter was sixteen she was sent back to Spain.

With Francisco's assassination in Peru, the Pizarro family lost favour with the Spanish throne and the eldest of the half-brothers, Hernando Pizarro, who had gone back to Spain to solicit aid for his brother from Charles V, was imprisoned in a castle in Medina del Campo. Since Hernando was a respected and wealthy man he was permitted a staff of servants and many liberties in his luxurious prison, and when his young niece arrived from Peru, in order to be near her only living relative, he installed her very comfortably in the castle.

Before his release a year later he married, at the age of fifty-five, this young daughter of his brother Francisco. When the confiscated rights and fortunes of the Pizarro family were returned to them, the couple went back to Trujillo to build a glorious palace and to found a noble line with their combined wealth from the New World.

Their intriguing palace is found in the north-east corner of the plaza and is easily recognizable, not only because of the intricate border of designs depicting the different months of the year which can be seen round the eaves, but because on the picturesque corner balcony which looks out on to the plaza, Pizarro and his wife placed their stone busts. One can still see the winsome little lace mantilla resting lightly on the little girl's simple coiffure, with its hanging ringlets. Francisco's daughter inherited her father's title of Marqués de la Conquista, and this little half-Incan Princess became the mother of a long line of Estremanians.

(It is amusing to note that when Charles V decided to give a title to Pizarro for his sensational discoveries in the New World, he sent a Royal Order to him, in which he said that he was giving him 'The Marquisate of whatever is the name of the place in which you find yourself'. Rather than call himself Marqués de Lima, or Cuzco, Pizarro called himself Marqués de la Conquista, and his followers got into the habit of calling him by that title, which his descendants carry today.)

I have found references to the magnificent jewels owned by this first mistress of the palace of Pizarro. Her emerald necklaces and headpieces were said to be made of stones of the most incredible size and splendour, and her great pearl necklaces and bracelets were set in heavy Indian gold. She obviously had a fabulous amount of precious jewels from the New World, because historians have all remarked on their beauty.

During the fifteenth and sixteenth centuries the Estremanian villages of Medellin and Trujillo were very united through frequent intermarriage of their noble families. In 1485 Hernan Cortes was born in Medellin of a Trujillan mother, Catalina Pizarro y Altamirano. Cortes as a child spent much time at his grandparents' palace in Trujillo, where he became a friend of his cousin Francisco Pizarro. He spent one year at the University of Salamanca where his head became so full of dreams of the New World that he left and signed up at the age of nineteen, in 1504, on a caravel leaving Seville for Santo Domingo. With his quick intelligence and control over men he soon distinguished himself in the new colony. When an expedition of two boats was sent from Santo Domingo to explore countries to the south-west, Cortes took over during a mutiny and on arrival in Mexican territory directed his followers successfully through several encounters with the natives.

Later he landed in Vera Cruz, Mexico, with ten caravels which he ordered burnt to make it impossible for his men to desert. This daring action obliged the soldiers to fight with the utmost valour and was one of the decisive steps in his conquest. Cortes captured the great Mexican Emperor Montezuma but his considerate treatment of this royal prisoner showed great justice.

Cortes married a Spanish woman from Santa Domingo called Catalina Juarez. Once he was installed in the palace of Montezuma she at least was able to join him, but she had great difficulty accustoming herself to the climate of Mexico City because she suffered from asthma.

Catalina was an extremely jealous woman and her husband's flirtations with the Indian maidens he received as booty gave her every reason to be so. One night during dinner Cortes, who usually did his best to conceal the strained relations between his wife and himself, made some remark to Catalina to silence her bickerings about his romantic activities which caused her to get up from the table and run out of the room. Cortes remained calmly with their guests for some two hours and then retired. The rest of the story has been reported by a palace servant and recorded in history.

When Cortes reached his apartments he found his wife kneeling and crying in front of a statue of the Virgin. In a few moments her maid prepared her señora for bed and Cortes was aided by his valet as was his custom. Several hours later, at about half past three in the morning, Cortes came out of his bedroom calling to his wife's servants to come immediately.

'I believe the Señora is dead!'

When Catalina's maid appeared, she found her mistress in bed in the arms of Cortes with a broken necklace around her neck and dark black marks on her throat. Cortes was in his lifetime accused and acquitted of assassinating his wife but many historians still claim this possibility.

The Conqueror of Mexico planned a return to Spain in 1528 when he was forty-three years old to request of Charles V a greater jurisdiction over Mexican affairs. He offered a free passage to Spain to any men who might want to make the trip and requested they bring with them as many Mexican rarities as possible. Cortes landed at the Spanish port of La Rabida with an enormous cortège of followers and surprises from the New World. He brought with him everything interesting and beautiful and unique that he had found on his trips. There were quantities of Indian warriors and Indian women, many tropical birds and animals, bars of gold, precious stones and hand-woven silks of bright colours and design.

During this visit he met the Mendoza sisters, two women very influential in the court of Charles V. He paid them much court and presented them with lovely gifts from the New World. Francisca, the younger of the two, interpreted these attentions to mean that Cortes was courting her in marriage and when she discovered that he was betrothed to another lady her fury led her to speak against him to Charles V. As a result, the king did not give Cortes the one distinction that he most coveted, the appointment of Viceroy of New Spain, despite the fact that he had bestowed upon this conquistador many honours, among them the title of Marqués del Valle.

Cortes returned disheartened to his new country, where he dedicated himself principally to developing an enormous farm and introducing new agricultural methods.

In 1540 he returned once more to his native land to complain again against the usurpation of his rights in Mexico. On this voyage Cortes brought with him his best-loved illegitimate son, Luis, who was about twelve, and his legitimate son Martin, who was then eight years old.

He was destined never to return to Mexico, and died in Seville on December 2, 1547, exhausted from the delays and difficulties of pleading his cause for seven years and desperately homesick for his new land.

One of the first Spaniards to influence Francisco Pizarro in the New World and the one who embarked him upon the idea of making an exploration south into the land of the Incas was Vasco Nuñez de Balboa. Nuñez de Balboa was born in 1475 in the Estremanian city of Badajoz. His soldiers not only admired and respected him, but they adored him with a blind faith in his every word and order. He picked up the Indian language with an astonishing quickness and was able to penetrate into the wildest areas of savage Indian tribes and to make them his friends. He learned from the natives that there was a great ocean to the west, and, against the advice of all, he dared to set out to discover the truth of this information. He and his men crossed the isthmus of Panama in 1513 carrying their nine ships on their shoulders, a feat for which many historians consider him greater than either Pizarro or Hernan Cortes. This enabled him to make explorations along the Pacific coast of Mexico and southern California which until then had been completely unknown to white men.

Two small cities were founded on that coast by the men who had followed Balboa. The people of these villages requested Charles V to name Nuñez de Balboa governor of that region which he had discovered. Balboa, who had dreams of new discoveries, was not interested in the governorship, but nevertheless he incurred the jealousy of a Spaniard called Pedrarias who was governor of a near-by area. This avaricious Spaniard imprisoned and condemned him to death with five of his most faithful followers. Francisco Pizarro, then a simple soldier in the ranks allotted to Pedrarias, was one of Nuñez de Balboa's prison guards in the days before his execution. Pizarro suffered greatly at this injustice to his old friend and from that moment on decided that he would make discoveries on his own instead of being dependent upon an ambitious superior.

The people of the small towns of Acla and Darien clamoured for the release of their hero but he was beheaded in the plaza of Acla at five o'clock one summer afternoon.

APPENDIX B

Among the most interesting Loaisa ancestors that I discovered in those manuscripts were the following:

There was Alvaro's cousin, Jeronimo, who went to the New World in 1525 as a young missionary priest and later became the first Archbishop of Lima, Peru. His experiences among the dangerous native tribes in areas where no white men had set foot before were recorded carefully in the old papers. Later, Jeronimo Loaisa founded the first university in the New World, the University of Lima and he also founded the first hospital, which exists in Lima today and bears his name.

There was also an uncle, Jofre de Loaisa, who had been Ambassador to the Sultan in Turkey and who had spent a great part of his life on the high seas defending Spain's merchant fleet from pirates.

In 1525 Charles V named this Loaisa as admiral of the first Spanish expedition around the world. Magellan, a Portuguese, had left the year before on a similar expedition but as yet news of his success had not reached the Peninsula.

The fleet under the command of the Admiral Loaisa left from La Coruna later that year and aboard the flag-ship travelled Sebastian de Elcano, the greatest mariner of the Spanish Conquest. The trip was uneventful until arriving near the tip of South America where bad weather was encountered. Some of the ships of the fleet were blown into a straits where the Portuguese, Magellan, had been forced the year before, but Jofre, wishing to make a complete turn, ventured to sail round the unknown cape, which he named Cabo Deseado. A devastating storm isolated his boat from the rest. Three ships had already been crippled; but the exhausted seamen, after great difficulties finally managed to bring what remained of the fleet into the calm waters of the Pacific.

Two months later without having discovered more than the coasts of Chile, the old Admiral died, the victim of illnesses which had come upon him due to the hardships of the voyage.

A young cousin from Trujillo called Alonso de Loaisa went to the New World at the age of seventeen where he distinguished himself in battle and later married the daughter of a brave Spanish captain. During the wedding celebrations their house was attacked, and in the ensuing battle the groom received a blow from an arquebus which completely removed one half of his face.

Alonso lived many years and became the founder of a long line of Loaisas in Peru. The old stories explain that his food had to be cut up like a child's, since he could not chew, and that to look upon him was truly a dreadful experience. At the end of his life Alonso and his wife Maria de Ayala, returned to Trujillo. They were buried in the side chapel which they had constructed in the small and lovely thirteenth century church of Santiago, and one can today see the two tombs in the wall and the carving which reads:

'This chapel was ordered to be built by Diego Alonso de Tapia, who in glory rests and Dona Maria Luisa S.V.M.V.G. It was erected to the glory of Jesus Christ and was completed in the year 1556.'

Here, as in succeeding instances throughout this story the reader might be confused by the same individual being referred to by different surnames. Likewise a son might be referred to by a surname different from that of his father. This is explained by the fact that medieval Spaniards retained the surnames of a father, mother and grandparents on both sides with equal respect and pride. In some cases a man would use his father's surname, whereas in other cases he would take advantage of the proud surname of a near ancestor.

In this particular case Alonso Loaisa, in preparing the chapel which was to hold his tomb, referred to himself as Diego Alonso de Tapia, Tapia being his grandmother's surname, a name extremely illustrious in Trujillo.

Another cousin, Garcia de Loaisa, was one of the outstanding ecclesiastics of his period and one of the few who dared to speak openly against the Inquisition. He was confessor to Charles V and later became head of the Council of the Indies, the government organization controlling Spanish possessions in the New World.

This fearless prelate went to Rome to attempt to secure the freedom of the Archbishop of Toledo, who was rotting in jail in the Vatican, after being condemned by the Spanish Inquisition. Loaisa, who believed sincerely that this old man was no heretic, managed to secure his release. During this time he discovered in Rome a young Greek painter and commissioned him to paint an altar piece for a church in Toledo. At Loaisa's instigation the young artist travelled to Toledo where he spent the rest of his days immortalizing that city whose inhabitants referred to him as 'El Greco'.

A BRIEF HISTORY OF THE GOLFINS

Sometime in the tenth century a family of French warriors called Delfin came into Spain to help fight against the advancing Arab armies. They were prominent in skirmishes in and near Toledo and by the eleventh century were completely acclimatized to the life of banditry and guerrilla warfare that was then prevalent in all isolated country districts in the Iberian peninsula. In order to provide themselves with the means of subsistence they were obliged to plunder and rob where they could, since law and order in the Moslem-controlled domains was almost non-existent in that period.

They elected from among themselves a king who founded a dynasty and who reigned with absolute authority. During the eleventh, twelfth and thirteenth centuries this powerful band, who were now called the Golfins, controlled and terrorized the greater part of Estremadura. They attacked principally the Moors: however, the Christian subjects of the king did not escape their assaults. Trujillo was the principal area affected, being situated nearest to the mountains of La Jara and Villuarcas, where the Golfins had built their guard-houses and their castles like eagles' nests on the highest mountain peaks. On almost every hill throughout Estremadura there were watch-towers controlled by the Golfins, which sent their messages from one area to another. So great was the danger from these bands that many inhabitants

Appendices

fled, and during a period of three hundred years the towns and villages under their yoke were in a constant state of terror. Successive Spanish kings offered rewards to noblemen who would raise forces to fight the Golfins, and inhabitants of Trujillo were the most active in trying to resist their attacks.

About 1260 the young king of the Golfins was a man called Alfon Golfin, noted for his bravery and audacity. In some unexplained way he met and fell in love with the daughter of the Mayor of Caceres. The attraction of this young lady was sufficient to induce Alfon Golfin to give up his life of banditry and to submit to the Spanish monarch of that time. Thus he married into the Estremanian nobility and built an elaborate palace in Caceres, renouncing for ever his life of banditry and adventure. Although bands of Golfins continued to terrorize the country up to the fourteenth century, from this moment on their destructive powers were greatly reduced.

When Alfon Golfin settled in Caceres he constructed an impressive fortress-palace typical of those times, with the busts of himself and his wife sculpted in stone on the façade, together with the family *escudo*. It was he who placed over the entrance to the palace this inscription carved in stone:

ESTA ES LA CASA DE LOS GOLFINES.

making his the only house in Caceres which announces in words as well as by the *escudo* its ownership.

Throughout the Middle Ages it was customary to take the surname of the wife in cases where it was the more illustrious. But the fact that Alfon Golfin not only kept his notorious surname, but that he had it carved in stone above the portal of his home, shows his pride in belonging to a clan who, although outlaws, had outwitted all Estremadura for two hundred and fifty years.

In the third generation we find that Pedro Alonso Golfin and his wife Inez Alvarez had three children. The first son, Alonso, continued in the house of his ancestors, bearing the title of Lord of Torre Arias. The second son, Garcia Golfin, with the title of

Appendices

Lord of Casa Corchada, built a palace on the hill above, and these two branches of the family were from then on referred to as 'The Golfins Down Below' and 'The Golfins Up Above'.

I mention this detail since both houses can be seen today in Caceres and might confuse anyone who took the trouble to visit them.

The third son, called Pedro Alonso like his father, married a girl from the wealthy Escobar family and took their last name from then on, as was often customary in those days with younger sons. In the fourth generation Alonso Golfin married Elena Figueroa from Llerena, a small town in the south-west tip of Estremadura, and to this couple was born another Alonso who became a Court official of Queen Isabella the Catholic.

At the end of the fifteenth century the head of the Golfin family was one Alonso Golfin, who married a Trujillian lady from the rich and distinguished family of Paredes. She was the eldest of a family of daughters and when she gave birth to her first child she named him Sancho after her father, with the understanding that the child would become his heir. However, several years later her father, then in his seventies, had a son who grew up to be the great Spanish warrior Diego Garcia de Paredes. Thus the family Golfin was thwarted in its hopes of joining all the Paredes wealth to that of their own.

Next to the *palacio* Alonso Golfin had constructed a convent to provide a chapel in which all the Golfins could have their family tombs, and over the entrance he ordered carved in stone, with the same arrogance as his forebears, the time-defying legend:

HERE THE GOLFINS AWAIT
THE DAY OF JUDGMENT.

Sancho de Golfin, his son, constructed a hall of arms within the fortress-palace in the form of a rectangular room around which he had placed the *escudo* of each head of family and his wife from the year 1262, allowing space for many future generations of Golfins.

Sancho de Golfin was born in the Casa de los Golfines about

1463 and at eighteen he joined Queen Isabella's troops and accompanied her for thirteen years, routing the Moors out of their last strongholds in Granada.

Sancho married the lady-in-waiting to the Queen and they had eighteen children, all of whom enjoyed the protection of the Queen and received important positions at Court. And the Queen named Sancho her Chamberlain or *camerero*, thereby making him the most powerful man in the country.

After the conquest of Granada, Queen Isabella began to occupy herself with the internal problems of the country and went to Caceres to spend several months in the Casa de los Golfines. For this reason a large carved stone *escudo* of the kings of Spain was placed above the door and is still there today. This was a customary privilege given wherever the kings were lodged.

While she was staying in the Casa de los Golfines the Queen signed many important documents relative to the discoveries in the New World, which today are included in the Golfin family archives.

The Golfin archives are in the possession of the Marqués de Santa Marta. One of the most interesting documents is the inventory of Queen Isabella's daughter Katherine's dowry when she left for England to marry Henry VIII.

Isabella died in 1504 at Medina del Campo and Sancho never left her side during the three months before her death. He was one of the witnesses to her testament. He held his post with the crown for more than forty years after her death. And when Sancho died in 1547 he was buried in the convent constructed by his father in Caceres.

In the manuscripts and books I had already come across references to a convent constructed by Alonso Golfin in 1493 and finished by his son Sancho. It seemed to give many headaches to its successive owners. In the year 1743 the nuns of this convent decided to substitute the altarpiece by another whose cost would be covered by the family of a nun of their order and which would bear the *escudo* of her family. Garcia Golfin y Carvajal, the head of the family at that time, opposed this and entered into a lawsuit. The nuns denied the existence of the patronage which had begun with Alonso Golfin in 1493 and they further denied that all the *escudos* of the doors and tombs which were found in that chapel belonged to the family Golfin.

The nuns lost the case because the family Golfin proved full rights, since they had never permitted the burial in the chapel of anyone not of their family. However, the centuries-long efforts of the Golfins to fight off the many attempts to confiscate the family mausoleum and chapel were finally frustrated in 1871 when the family lost its last lawsuit over this convent.

And so the city of Caceres took possession of this convent and the burial grounds of the Golfins. That proud prophecy, 'HERE THE GOLFINS AWAIT THE DAY OF JUDGMENT', was pulled down and dumped in the patio of the Golfin *palacio*. All the tombs of the Golfins were opened and the ancient caskets were removed and deposited in the Golfin home. Later that year the building of the new town hall was constructed on that site.

Meanwhile the head of the family ordered the general reburial of the disinterred ancestors, but oddly enough one casket remained in the house, where it was removed to a corner of the library. That casket held the bones of the great Sancho de Golfin.

Several years later the family library was moved to Madrid where the Golfin descendants now lived most of the year. Inadvertently the bones of Sancho were shipped along with the other effects. It was Miguel Canilleros who told me that undoubtedly Sancho's casket was in the library of Luis' uncle's home in Madrid.

'I feel certain that probably no one is aware of the fact,' Miguel added. 'My conscience will not be at ease until I have arranged a respectable burial in the cathedral of Caceres for the greatest of all the Golfins.'

I thought that perhaps old Sancho might be just as pleased to remain in the family library side by side with the familiar books and with the good central heating in the winter. I was remembering the icy stone floor of the cathedral in Caceres, which was evidently the spot my friend had in mind for him.

'Undoubtedly Alfonso Santa Marta, your uncle, will gladly ship the body back to Caceres once I inform him it is resting in his library, but I am not at all sure he will be willing to make the trip himself to attend the ceremony. We must have someone from the family present and you could be that person.'

It seemed to me that the very powerful and distinguished Sancho might have every reason to be indignant that I would be the only one to represent his descendants, but the wrath of the dead being easy to bear, I was more than willing to do this if it pleased my friend.

'But Miguel, why do you think the body of Sancho was not reburied with the others in 1871?'

'Well,' he surmised, 'Sancho, being undoubtedly the most distinguished of the Golfin lineage, might have been buried separately from the others, and the family might have preserved his casket with the thought in mind of giving him a more ceremonious burial when time permitted. Or the remains of Sancho might have been found in a better state of preservation than those of his relatives.,

'For example,' Miguel went on 'in the cases where I have been present at the opening of centuries-old caskets in Caceres, little remained in the interior other than dust, sometimes accompanied by a metal button or a ring. Even the clothes in which the corpse had been dressed had completely crumbled with time. However, in rare cases, where perhaps the body had been by some chance hermetically sealed, the person remained completely intact.'

This did not prove to be true in Sancho's case. Miguel discovered that Sancho's remains were not exactly in a coffin. In fact, they were in a small box about the size of a shoebox.

'Obviously,' said Miguel, 'when they dug up the body years ago, all they found were these pieces—a rather well-preserved skull, several thigh bones, rib bones and a pelvic bone.'

Miguel asked permission to transfer the remains and arrange

for a proper burial in the cathedral and so the box was sent to the Conde de Canilleros covered with black velvet with a large white cross in the centre. Permission was granted by the bishop to hold the funeral and so at last Sancho returned to his final resting place in Caceres.

BIBLIOGRAPHY

Trujillo—Sus Hijos y Monumentos, Clodoaldo Naranjo

Guia Historica-Artistica de Caceres, Antonio C. Floriano

Cronicas Trujillanas del Siglo XVI, Miguel Muñoz de San Pedro

Historia de Peru, Carlos Zavala Cyague

Nuñez de Balboa, Octavio Mendez Pereira

Los Descargos del Emperador, Excom. Sr. Antonio Marichalar Marqués
de Montesa

Diego Garcia de Paredes, Miguel Munoz de San Pedro

Hernan Cortez, Salvador de Madariaga

A History of Spain, Rafael Altamira

Historia de la Casa de Lara, Salazar y Castro

Francisco Pizarro, Luis Manrique

Castillos de España, Mauche

Ayuntamiento y Familias Cacerenses, Public Lentado Caceres 1915–1918

Memoirs on Reign of Louis XIV and the Regency, Saint Simon

Caceres bajo la Rena Catolica y su Camerero Sancho de Paredes Golfin,
Miguel Orti Belmonte

San Francisco de Borja, Amarie Dennis

Highlights of Spanish History, Richard C. Harris

El Greco y Toledo, G. Maranon

Felipe II, W. Thomas Walsh

MANUSCRIPTS

Fifty untranslated manuscripts from the archives of Caceres.

Three manuscripts from the archives of the village of Santa Marta.

One hundred manuscripts from the archives of the Marqués de Santa
Marta.

Thirty manuscripts from the archives of Trujillo.

PASCUALETE HISTORY   SEPTEMBER 22- 2011

Sixty years later

Never have I reread one of my books after it was published, but yesterday I picked up this old book and began to read. Since I had described with exactitude the details of my first visit and those years when I was struggling to make that old home livable, as I read I felt again the charm and beauty of Extremadura's agricultural world of so long ago. I realized, as I have many times before, how fortunate I was to have been living in Pascualete during those years when the people still lived as farmers had in centuries before the transition to mechanized farming as it is today. When I arrived in Pascualete in 1950 the country was one century behind the rest of Europe. In Madrid when I arrived in 1944, as yet no automobiles were made in Spain - not even electric refrigerators or any other electrical equipment was fabricated. The few automobiles in the big cities had all been imported from other European countries.

Today I enjoy, as we all do, cell phones, television, good highways, but having experienced in the early fifties the charm of the life of farmers with no electricity or running water, I am aware that our ancestors enjoyed pleasures and human relationships perhaps more meaningful than our modern life offers today.

However in the year 1964 everything changed abruptly when agricultural equipment began to arrive in Extremadura for the first time. This modernization brought disaster for the majority of our employees who remained without work, as other agricultural employees in the province. Many emigrated to the city of Madrid where industrialization had just begun, others to Germany where work was available. No longer would I see oxen filing into the patio after a day's labor in the fields, nor were donkeys arriving with employees from Santa Marta – little by little a few small Spanish made automobiles would arrive with the few people for whom we still had some work . Even Pillete moved to Madrid for short visits, his daughter opened a restaurant carrying his name in the Plaza of Trujillo. The chozos disappeared entirely since we built houses for the employees with modern conveniences. In the beginning it was difficult to convince our reduced number of shepherds to live in normal small houses - they preferred the chozos - they did not like the modern conveniences we provided and complained bitterly saying that chozos were much healthier places to live. A large majority of men in Santa Marta were without work, as were their children. Fortunately I was able to send many young Santa Marta men to Paris to work as servants for our friends the Dukes of Windsor, the Barons of Rothschild and others. They were a great success and finally I sent nine young men from Santa Marta to Paris. After saving enough money two of them returned and established profitable businesses which make them today the outstanding families of the town. The daughter of Maria and Primitive married my new chauffeur. Pepe married one of the many girls who pursued him and eventually came to own a gasoline station on the outskirts of Madrid.

However we continued to come to Pascualete for Holy week vacations and Christmas and many weekends in the fall and winter with friends to shoot partridge, but nothing were as wonderful for me as it had been before.

Yet when we brought Audrey Hepburn, the famous cinema star and her husband, Mel Ferrer, to Pascualete for a Holy-week vacation about 1966, they were enchanted with the medieval atmosphere of the house and the loved Trujillo. Audrey returned several times with her little son Sean, then about four years old, who enjoyed playing with the baby sheep just as my children had.

And a few years later, the Maharaja of Jaipur and his wife Ayesha were fascinated with Pascualete and the town of Santa Marta as well when they came to visit. Jai, (his nickname) said the town reminded him of his small villages in Jaipur. My husband must have had some family sense of loyalty for that pueblo because later, when we were alone, he surprised me, saying that Santa Marta was certainly more attractive than any small town in India. The Maharaja was then Indian Ambassador to Spain and returned many times to shoot partridge with us during those years.

Nevertheless the history of Trujillo and its heroes also always interested me. Although we never formed another group to attempt to uncover the remains of Diego Garcia de Paredes, he is still remembered by Trujillans - his fame as a physical giant and as King Charles the Fifth's bravest and most outstanding officer used to be celebrated every year by a "running of the bulls" in the plaza, and his daring exploits are a story proud Trujillans tell their children. But other heroes of Trujillo became more known worldwide. The famous American benefactress, Mrs. Huntington, contracted the important sculptor, Charles Cary Rumsey, to do a statue of Pizarro which she donated to Trujillo - today it is a spectacular sight in the center of the city's main plaza. She also had another similar statue of Pizarro made for Lima to honor him in the city he founded in Peru.

Although Hernan Cortez, discoverer of Mexico, was born in a town near Trujillo, his statue can be seen in Caceres. Actually during the medieval centuries Trujillo was a larger and more important city than Caceres and can boast of a larger number of conquistadores. The French destruction of Trujillo at the beginning of the nineteenth century reduced the city's size and importance -   today it has a much smaller population than Caceres. But due to Golfin's success in keeping the French troops out of Caceres, the ancient part of that city remains intact and provides an outstanding example of the beauty of the cities of the Middle Ages.

Meanwhile over the years my desire to protect the beauty of the ancient city of Trujillo led me to invite friends to spend a few days in Pascualete and then to take them through the ancient parts of Trujillo, hoping they would appreciate the beauty of the city and buy and restore one of the old abandoned palaces. The first and most influential of all these friends were Javier Salas, then director of the Museum del Prado, and his wife Carmen- When visiting us in Pascualete they had become fascinated with Trujillo – very soon they bought and restored two important ruins. Also they helped me encourage other friends to restore ruined palacios which otherwise would have disappeared with time.

Luis and I started to invite foreign friends who we considered might be interested in Trujillo. Among them was Cornelius Vanderbilt Whitney, recently named USA Ambassador to Spain – he and his wife, Marylou, spent a week with us in Pascualete and agreed to buy one of the larger palaces – they had to return to the USA but said they would do this if I would take care of arranging the papers and permits. This was not easy- it obliged me to investigate the owners of past centuries to find the present owner, but finally after a year of constant efforts, I was able to buy the palace for them.   When they decided to bring an American decorator to furnish the palace, I convinced them to employ Duarte Pinto Coelho, a Portuguese friend, who was then trying to establish himself in Spain as a decorator. Another longtime American friend, currently living in London and an artist of repute, Fleur Cowles, visited us and fell in love with two towers of an ancient a palace which she bought and repaired.

A sojourn in Pascualete also encouraged our cousin, the Marquesa de Santa Cruz to prepare an apartment for herself in her huge palace which was currently occupied and protected by nuns. But by the 1970's Trujillo had gained much renown. Carmen Salas and I realized that a formal legal process and an official document would be necessary to protect the city, its ancient buildings and it's immediate surroundings. Therefore on January 14th 1971 we organized the first meeting of the Board of the Association of AMIGOS DE TRUJILLO. My husband was named president; Javier Salas vice-president, Carmen secretary and I became the publicity manager along with a long list of distinguished Spaniards who were members of the Board. Within a short time the Association of AMIGOS DE TRUJILLO obtained government approval and aid. Today it remains a source of permanent protection for the city of Trujillo.

During a visit to America in 1979 in either Pitttsburg or maybe it was Philadelphia in the state of Pennsylvania where I had just given one of my many conferences to a large audience, a city official informed me that in the city's main art museum was an excellent portrait of a Countess of Quintanilla done by Goya. This man was aware that Quintanilla was a title I had been using until recently. When he saw that I was incredulous, he insisted upon taking me to the Museum to view the painting. I was certain he had made a mistake but when later I stood in front of the impressive portrait, I realized that probably this was one of the many objects the French soldiers had robbed during their destruction of Trujillo from either the Casa de la Boveda or another family palace. Evidently the painting had passed from Trujillo to France and then to the Museum in Pennsylvania.

The pursuit of historical objects, houses, events and personalities is fascinating. Each one leads to a captivating story. The Count of Quintanilla in 1808 had been the uncle of the Marquesa de Santa Marta, mother of the unfortunate four sisters. On investigating further into the history of the Quintanilla title, I discovered that the story was a sad one. Precisely in 1808 during the first days of the French invasion, the Count of Quintanilla and two other distinguished men of Trujillo had been brutally murdered. His tomb and that of his wife are visible today in the cemetery of Trujillo – their title eventually passed on to us through my husband's grandfather, the son of the only daughter of the four sisters who had all died in childbirth. Our ancestors who inhabited Pascualete at the beginning of the nineteenth century suffered many atrocities from the French troops – these tragedies undoubtedly strengthened my husband´s brave ancestor, Pedro Cayetano Golfin, in his determination to save Caceres from a similar attack by the French army.

As time went on my children and grandchildren developed the same affection I felt for Extremadura, its people and their customs. They enjoy as I do the improvements and additions Trujillans have added to their city. The restaurant Coral del Rey offers a menu as superior as any in Madrid, the family Elias possesses one of the outstanding Spanish dress designers and he also founded a museum for fashion in Trujillo. And in contrast the city of Trujillo in 1951 when the mere appearance of an automobile created a mass of spectators today Trujillo has many large garages for automobiles.

Also located on the border of the city is one of Spain´s three horse centers, important internationally for training and for the sale of the famous   Spanish horse. The magnificent picadero is a contrast to the former picturesque sight of gypsies bartering the sale of horses during what used to be in that same area the yearly Animal Fair. These attractions have brought many tourists to the city which now has all the modern advantages but the Trujillans have been cautious to protect the beauty and grandness of the ancient city.

Tourists also are captivated by the countryside which possesses unusual birds, many of which are extinct in other European countries. Among them is the gigantic Avutarda – a bird of two meters and half width with a medium weight of fifteen kilos. Precisely Pascualete is in the center of this bird haven territory and in the spring large numbers of bird lovers from foreign countries come to our area with impressive specialized modern equipment to photograph and record every detail of the very special birds in our fields.

Extremadura is recognized as the last large agricultural area of all Europè with its ample open fields, forests of encinas and cork trees and olive groves. The large amounts of cattle, sheep, goats, and pigs contribute food for many parts of Europe. And added to the practical advantages of this outstanding province is the beauty of the wild expansive country which includes rivers and mountainous areas.

Pascualete has always produced sheep with an excellent quality of milk, due to the abundance of wild plants and herbs of rosemary and thyme. With this milk, the wives of our shepherds during centuries made an especially delicious cheese; the recipe has been passed from generation to generation.

My love for Extremadura, linked to my great attachment to Pascualete, its land and its people led me to start a new adventure. I suggested to my grandchildren to take these recipes of rich cheeses that we had enjoyed so many times when our shepherds offered them to us and to start producing them for public use. Today, thanks to the advances in agriculture and industry we can produce, several artisan cheeses containing delicious flavors.

I called old friends in France and Italy and asked them to put me in touch with the best cheese masters, inviting them to come and work with us, to teach us the latest techniques of how to make cheese, but remaining respectful of our traditional flavors. Our commitment was and still is to produce these recipes and to maintain maximum hygiene and quality. Many months' trials and efforts bore fruit and today we have a variety of wonderful Finca Pascualete cheeses.

When our friends came to hunt in Pascualete, or to enjoy the peace of our countryside, I often offered the different varieties of cheese the shepherds had given me. Today I offer my friends La Torta, el Cumbre de Trujillo and el Pascualino with truffle. I enjoy watching their reactions while we discuss the flavors they prefer. I am often surprised and learn much from their enlightening comments. Some say the cheese tastes like thyme and rosemary; others are especially attracted by the smell.

We produce the cheeses with great care in the process from beginning to end. We breed the best lambs, which will give the best milk and we select carefully the pieces we produce. Just as I liked to be with the shepherds in old times, now I enjoy accompanying the men in the factory, monitoring as I used to years ago.

Of our six different flavors, my favorite is our mini Torta - a delicious soft smooth cheese, agreeable to take with a spoon or spread on a cracker while sharing it with a friend – it even seems to make the conversation more agreeable.

Today my hope is that my descendants in Pascualete will contribute as their ancestors did during seven centuries to the prosperity of Extremadura and that they will also collaborate in developing many ways to add to the excellence and importance of this outstanding province, the most beautiful agricultural corner remaining today in Europe.

Made in the USA
San Bernardino, CA
18 August 2016